D0641042

Foundations of Modern Sociology Series

Alex Inkeles, *Editor*

Foundations of Modern Sociology Series

the sociology
of economic life

Neil J. Smelser, *University of California, Berkeley*

Prentice-Hall, Inc., *Englewood Cliffs, New Jersey*

Prentice-Hall Foundations of Modern Sociology Series

Alex Inkeles, *Editor*

Library of Congress Catalog No.: 63–18024.

Designed by Harry Rinehart

Current printing (last digit):

13 12 11 10 9 8 7 6 5 4

PRENTICE-HALL INTERNATIONAL, INC., *London*
PRENTICE-HALL OF AUSTRALIA, PTY., LTD., *Sydney*
PRENTICE-HALL OF CANADA, LTD., *Toronto*
PRENTICE-HALL FRANCE, S. A. R. L., *Paris*
PRENTICE-HALL OF INDIA PRIVATE LIMITED, *New Delhi*
PRENTICE-HALL OF JAPAN, INC., *Tokyo*
PRENTICE-HALL DE MEXICO, S. A., *Mexico City*

C-82126 (*p*), C-82127 (*c*)

preface

As its title reveals, this volume stands between two disciplines. My hope is that it may be a modest contribution to both. For economists, whose research often concerns the relations among economic variables alone, I hope the book will be a reminder of the importance of the social setting in which economic life is embedded. For sociologists, whose research on economic behavior is valuable but very scattered, I hope it will provide a coherent framework for assembling the results of this research.

In preparing these pages, I have been guided by several objectives. I have attempted to give a faithful and accurate representation—within the limitations of space—of the dominant traditions of thought and research in that borderline area between economics and sociology. I have attempted to be as comprehensive as possible—again within the same limitations—in covering these materials. And finally, I have tried to attain clarity of exposition without oversimplifying the necessarily complex ideas at hand.

I envision that this book, by virtue of its interdisciplinary character, may prove useful in several different kinds of courses: (1) For courses in sociology that now go under the title of "Industrial Sociology." The book provides a base for studying economic life in societies other than the industrial ones. (2) For courses in economic principles and organization. The book is an introduction to the social environment of economic behavior for the student of economics. (3) For courses in general education, which are concerned with

v

the relations among different traditions of knowledge. (4) For courses in applied subjects like business administration, which must view economic practices in their complex social setting.

In the early stages of preparing this book I carried on helpful conversations with Alfred H. Conrad of Harvard and with Frederick E. Balderston and Harvey Leibenstein of the University of California, Berkeley—all economists—on recent developments in economics that have raised sociological questions. During the summer of 1962, when the writing was in its later stages, Talcott Parsons of Harvard was visiting Berkeley; I benefited greatly from our long conversations on the many issues that arose from his readings of the manuscript. At every stage of my work the criticisms and suggestions of Alex Inkeles of Harvard, general editor of the Foundations of Modern Sociology Series, alerted me to new problems and ideas.

Marvin B. Scott of the University of California, Berkeley, who has taught me much about expressing myself clearly, provided many substantive and stylistic suggestions. The manuscript was processed efficiently, accurately, and with good cheer by Mrs. Pauline Ward and by the staff of the Institute of Industrial Relations, University of California, Berkeley.

Neil J. Smelser

contents

introduction

The Aim of This Book

To understand and predict any aspect of social life, we cannot ignore economic matters. Take political conflict as an example. A mining town in West Virginia is likely to face recurrent political battles over working conditions, consumer debt, and public welfare. The citizens of a suburban town outside Philadelphia are likely to be preoccupied with school issues, transportation to the metropolis, and tax rates. In a Florida tourist town political conflicts may focus on liquor-licensing, building permits, and the state of recreational facilities. In all three cases distinctive types of political conflict may be traced in part to distinctive economic differences.

Take friendship as another example. For any given industrial plant it is possible to predict many of a man's friendship choices fairly accurately by knowing where he stands in the economic division of labor. We frequently refer to "managerial cliques" and "workmen's cliques" to indicate that friendships form among those occupying similar positions in productive organizations.

In turn the non-economic aspects of social life affect the economic. By knowing the political conditions of different societies, for instance, it is possible to predict some of the economic activities that will occur in them. American investors traditionally have chosen to invest abroad either in politically stable areas (such as Canada or parts of Europe) or in areas over which the United States exercises strong political influence (such as Latin

1

America). By the same token, these investors shy away from less politically stable parts of the world, even though these areas may offer promising economic opportunities.

Even something so intimate as friendship may condition economic processes. If workmen in a clique do not accept management's goals of production, they often try deliberately to slow their output. Moreover, they use the lever of friendship and loyalty to enforce these restrictive practices in their group. Members often "go along" with the group norms because they wish to remain in good standing in the clique.

The social world, then, is made up of many aspects—economic, political, religious, familial, educational, and others—all of which can be defined independently of one another, but all of which influence one another in practice. Corresponding to these aspects are various branches of the social sciences. Economics and political science, for instance, concentrate more or less exclusively on the range of problems that arise in the economic and political areas, respectively. Sociology as a field covers a number of social aspects, as indicated by its sub-branches—sociology of religion, sociology of education, and so on.

This book concerns the economic aspect of life, but it is not a book on economics, as the term is generally employed. Rather, it is concerned with the relations between the economic and non-economic aspects of social life—how these aspects overlap, how they influence one another. We refer to this subject as "economic sociology."

Economic sociology has grown in shreds and patches. Its contributors go under many labels—economists, labor relations experts, industrial sociologists, industrial psychologists, demographers, economic anthropologists, and those who study in vaguely delimited areas known as the sociology of work, the sociology of leisure, the sociology of occupations, the sociology of formal organizations, and the sociology of economic development. Despite its diversity of origins, the common feature of economic sociology remains a preoccupation with the causal relations between the economic and non-economic aspects of social life.

In our aim to pull together some of these strands of thought and research, we shall ask three kinds of question:

1. What do we need to know in the field of economic sociology? What are the main issues in the field?

2. What do we actually know? What are the major findings of economic sociology? What confidence can we have in these findings?

3. What remains to be known? Do the findings of economic sociology have any genuine bearing on what we need to know in the field? What are the major "unknowns" in theory and empirical research?

The Program of This Book

We shall examine these questions from a number of different angles:

1. From the standpoint of the *history of thought*. In part, the history of *economic* thought is a procession of major figures who have made advances in discerning the workings of the economic system. In developing their economic ideas, however, these thinkers have made certain assertions about the non-economic aspects of life. Sometimes these assertions play a significant role in their economic theories. In Chapter 1 we shall examine some of the non-economic assumptions of Adam Smith,

Karl Marx, John Maynard Keynes, and others. We shall also glance at the history of *sociological* thought, represented by figures such as Émile Durkheim and Max Weber, who have inquired specifically into the relations among the economic and non-economic features of society. Finally, to locate the viable issues in modern economic sociology, we shall examine a few recent trends in economics, sociology, and anthropology.

2. From a *methodological* standpoint. In Chapter 2 we shall inspect economics and sociology as disciplines. We shall ask what kinds of scientific problem are posed in each field, what kinds of concept are used in each to attack these problems, and what kinds of explanation are generated in each. Then we shall be in a position to give a formal account of the distinctive character of economic sociology, and to set it off from related lines of inquiry.

3. From a *systemic* standpoint. Having examined economic sociology from the historical and methodological angles, we shall turn to the substance of the field in Chapter 3. Initially we shall consider the economy as a sub-system of society; then we shall ask how it is related to other major sub-systems—the cultural system (for example, values and ideologies), the political system, the stratification system, and so on. As we proceed, many of the findings of economic sociology will fall into place.

4. From the standpoint of *economic processes*. If we concern ourselves only with major social sub-systems and their relations, we remain at a very general level of discourse. To get a closer view of the impingement of non-economic variables on economic variables (and vice versa), we shall study the central economic processes in concrete detail in Chapter 4. We shall begin with the production of goods and services, then turn to distribution and exchange, and finally look at consumption.

5. From the standpoint of *economic and social change*. It is one thing to examine the findings of economic sociology with reference to production, distribution, and consumption *within* a given economic and social structure. It is quite another to study the relations among economic and social variables when the major structures in society are *changing*. We shall devote Chapter 5 to the relations between economic and social change, emphasizing the problems of adjustment faced by the new nations of the world.

historical developments in economic sociology

one

In the past two centuries many eminent thinkers have sought to cope with the major issues of economic sociology. To focus our attention on different strands of intellectual development, we shall consider the history of economic thought, then the history of sociological thought, and finally some recent developments in several disciplines.

Sociological Aspects of Economic Life as Revealed in Economic Thought

So rich is the history of economic thought, even in the past 200 years, that a full coverage of its non-economic implications would in itself require a volume. With only a few pages to devote to this subject, we shall simplify our task in three ways. First, we shall consider only a few major persons and schools. Second, we shall ignore the major economic significance of these thinkers and concentrate on the sociological by-ways of their thought. Third, among these sociological concerns, we shall restrict ourselves mainly to one non-economic dimension—the political. This restriction is not altogether unrealistic, for economics was called "political economy" through much of the nineteenth century.

Mercantilism

The concept of mercantilism refers to a heterogeneous body of ideas that dominated European economic thought during the seventeenth and eighteenth centuries. These ideas do not form a coherent economic theory, but a conglomeration of value judgments, policy recommendations, and assertions about the nature of economic life. The heterogeneity of mercantilism traces in part to the diversity of persons who espoused it—philosophers, heads of state, legislators, merchants, and pamphleteers. From this bewildering array, we may extract a few central themes.

The first theme concerns the mercantilists' view of wealth. The wealth of a country was held to be equal to the amount of money possessed by that country. Moreover, mercantilists identified the possession of money with the possession of the precious metals, gold, and silver. Since they conceived the total stock of wealth in the world as being more or less stationary, they felt that whatever one country gained in wealth, another country lost. (This view contrasts with the view held by modern economists that foreign trade often benefits both countries, even though one may run a deficit for a time.) Hence the mercantilists stressed the importance of either accumulating precious metals outright or maintaining a balance of exports over imports so that precious metals would flow into the home country.

The second theme concerns the mercantilists' view of power and its relation to wealth. One major way to increase national power, many felt, was to increase national wealth. As O. H. Taylor writes,

> In [the mercantilist epoch] . . . , the main over-all purpose of each country's government, in its efforts to stimulate and direct or guide the country's commerce and handicraft industries, was to foster growth of national wealth *mainly for the sake of* national diplomatic and military power and security. The main concern of each nation's policy was for growth of the relative wealth-and-power of the nation-state as such and as compared with rival, foreign nation-states. . . .[1]

Mercantilists assumed that wealth worked in the service of power, and that the objectives of increasing wealth and increasing power are in essential harmony, indeed almost indistinguishable from one another.

With respect to practical policy as well, mercantilists saw an intimate association between power and wealth. The state is the locus of power. To stimulate economic growth and the increase of wealth, the state should use this power to regulate industry and trade. It should give political and economic support—by establishing state monopolies, for instance—to industries that manufacture goods for export; it should restrict imports by taxation or prohibition; it should colonize both to acquire supplies of gold and silver and to secure raw materials to be worked up for export. By thus increasing its wealth, the state was also increasing its power.

From the standpoint of the status of economic and political variables, then, the mercantilists had an undifferentiated theory. By increasing wealth a state increases its power; moreover, it uses its power to increase wealth. If properly controlled, the economic system and the political system cannot work at cross-purposes; they are complementary aspects of one another.

[1] *A History of Economic Thought* (New York: McGraw-Hill, 1960), p. 82.

Adam Smith

Adam Smith (1723–1790) was the foremost critic of the mercantilist doctrines. From the multi-sided polemic scattered through his famous *Wealth of Nations*,[2] we may extract the following attacks on and reformulations of the basic themes of mercantilism.

With respect to the nature of wealth, Smith forcefully rejected the mercantilists' emphasis on money or treasure. The wealth of a nation, he argued, is to be found in the productive base of the nation, or its power to produce "the necessaries, comforts and conveniences of life." Money is a medium of exchange that facilitates the allocation of these goods. The level of production depends in turn on the economic division of productive labor. The more highly specialized is labor, the more productive it is. The level of specialization of labor depends in its turn on the size of the markets for the products of labor and the availability of capital. If the market is wide and the supply of capital is abundant, the economy can build and maintain an advanced division of labor.

Because Smith's theory of wealth diverged so radically from that of the mercantilists, he denied the importance of accumulating a treasure of precious metals. Rather, to increase wealth, it is necessary to work for the widest possible markets for distributing products. This reasoning lies behind his argument for maximum international trade to be attained by freeing it from tariffs and other restrictions.

Smith also revised the mercantilists' ideas regarding the relations between wealth and power. While not denying that a nation's power depends in part on its wealth, he attacked the notion that the best way to increase national wealth is through specific political encouragement. Governments should not establish monopolies, fix tariffs, or show favoritism to certain industries. Rather they should allow the power to make economic decisions to *reside in the hands of the economic agents themselves*. In terms of power, the famous doctrine of *laissez faire* means that the state should not regulate, but should give business and commercial agents the power to regulate themselves. Strictly speaking, then, *laissez faire* means a reallocation of power in the social system, not simply an absence of power.

Such a decentralization of power does not, however, solve all the political problems of a system. What guarantees that individual economic agents will not misuse their power and gain control of the market, fix prices, and so on? Smith attempted to handle this problem by two devices:

1. He built into his theory an assumption that has become one of the core elements of the classical ideal of the "perfectly competitive market"— the assumption that no individual firm has (or should have) the power to influence price or total output of an industry. In this kind of model, power is ruled out as a variable. No economic agent can at the same time be a political agent. Smith realized that in practice businessmen and others agreed to pool their power in order to regulate prices and output; persons "in the same trade seldom meet together," he said, "but the conversation ends in a conspiracy against the public." But he felt these agreements were unnatural and illegitimate. If the economy were completely free, business-

---

[2] First published in 1776. An inexpensive modern edition is Adam Smith, *Inquiry into the Nature and Causes of the Wealth of Nations* (New York: The Modern Library, 1937).

historical developments in economic sociology

men would devote their capital to the most productive enterprises, and the shares of income would find their "natural" level in the market. The economy would regulate itself.

Smith applied the same reasoning to international trade. He urged that individual nations not make use of their power in creating monopolies for exporters or erecting tariffs. Each country would produce that which was relatively most profitable in terms of its resources, and through free international trade an optimum allocation of goods would result.

2. He assumed that certain very general political constraints must operate to prevent businessmen from pursuing their self-interest in a completely unbridled way. For instance, the state would provide a legal framework to guarantee that sales and contracts would be honored; the state would *not* grant favors to special groups in the economy. Thus even under *laissez-faire* assumptions, the state is not completely passive. It provides a moral, legal, and institutional setting that encourages business in general but not particular business enterprises.

Karl Marx

The thought of Karl Marx (1818–1884) is extremely complex, in part because he attempted to synthesize so many varied lines of intellectual influence that converged on him—especially German idealism, French socialism, and British economics. Hence we can give here only the barest sketch of his view of economics and society, with special reference to his assertions about political forces.

According to Marx, every society, whatever its stage of historical development, rests on an economic foundation. Marx called this foundation the "mode of production" of commodities. The mode of production in turn has two components. The first is "the forces of production," or the physical and technological arrangement of economic activity. The second component of the mode of production is "the social relations of production" or the indispensable human attachments that men must form with one another in carrying on this economic activity. The mode of production as a whole Marx called "the economic structure of society."

But society is composed of more than its productive arrangements. Resting on the economic structure is what Marx referred to as "superstructure" or that complex of legal, political, religious, aesthetic, and other institutions.

> The totality of [the] relations of production constitutes the economic structure of society—the real foundation, on which legal and political superstructures. . . . The mode of production . . . determines the general character of the social, political, and spiritual processes of life.[3]

This dependency might work out in the following way: The most fundamental set of social relations that emerge from the process of production is a class structure, or the division of society into a powerful wealthy class and a weak poor class. Under the capitalist mode of production—Marx analyzed the capitalist system in greatest detail—the two classes are the bourgeoisie and the proletarians. The bourgeoisie constitute the class that owns the means of production, directs the productive process, and reaps

[3] Karl Marx, *Critique of Political Economy* (New York: International Library, 1904), p. 11.

the profits from it; the proletarians are wage-workers who perform the actual labor but who do not receive full rewards for their labor. Given these relations of production, we would expect the state, the church, the community— in short, the superstructure—to operate in the service of the bourgeoisie and help keep the workers subordinate. For instance, politicians and the armed forces would keep down worker discontent, and religious leaders would feed ideologies to the masses to convince them either that they are not oppressed or that they will be saved in a future life.

Let us now examine the relations between economic and political forces in particular. Marx assumed that the capitalist has access to power because of his position in the economic system; he owns the means of production, and he buys the laborers' services. The worker, on the other hand, has only his labor to sell, and only wages given in return. Because of his superior position, the capitalist is able to exploit the worker by lengthening the work day, forcing his wife and children to work, speeding up the machinery, and displacing the worker by installing more productive machinery. The capitalist's power is buttressed, furthermore, by the existence of political authorities who pass laws detrimental to the workers and put down their attempts to protest through rioting, striking, and demonstrating. Under such circumstances the political forces in society work in the service of the economic forces; or, we might say, the political sector stands in a *positive functional relation* to the economic.

This, however, is not the whole story. Marx maintained that the positive functional relation is not an enduring one. In fact, each type of economic system contains what Marx called "the seeds of its own destruction." Under capitalism, for instance, the bourgeoisie, driven by competition and other forces to maintain and increase their profits, gradually drive the workers more and more into misery and desperation. These conditions are exaggerated by the occurrence of increasingly severe economic depressions. How do the workers respond? At first they react irrationally by rioting and destroying machinery. After a time, however, they begin to become more politically aware, they join unions, agitate for limitations on the length of the working day, join cooperative societies, and so on. Finally, at the height of their maturity, the workers forge a genuinely revolutionary party which rises to destroy the entire capitalist system and usher in a socialist one.

What does this process imply in terms of the relations between economic and political forces in society? It means that as the workers become more and more threatening, the political forces are no longer working in the service of the economic. In fact they threaten to destroy the economic system. The political forces now cease to be positively functional, and become *disfunctional*. Indeed, it is through political revolution, not economic action, that the workers accomplish the destruction of capitalism.

Marx, then, had a complex view of the relations between economic and political forces. In the vital phases of the development of an economic system, the political arrangements consolidate the economic arrangements; in the degenerative phases the economic and political forces come into conflict, and this conflict leads ultimately to the doom of the system. In the Marxian system, no alternative solution is possible. At any given time, then, the exact functional relations between the economic and political forces depend on the stage of development of the society in question.

8

The Study of Imperfect Competition

In reviewing Adam Smith's assumptions about power, we noted that he established the beginnings of the model of the perfectly competitive market—the market in which no individual firm has the power to control price or output. Under such market conditions, those firms that price too high, produce too much, or operate inefficiently are forced either to come into line with the existing conditions of production or go out of business. This model has occupied a prominent place in the history of economic thought. By the early twentieth century, theory based on these assumptions had reached a high point of development.

Clearly, however, not all actual market conditions approximate the model of perfect competition. For one reason or another, a few agents may rise to a position of power and influence conditions of output or price. If one or two sellers control all the supply of a given product—sulfur, for instance—they can call the tune because buyers cannot turn to alternative sources. If the product—again, sulfur might be an example—has no substitutes, the sellers possess an advantage, again because buyers have limited alternatives. Finally, if a government establishes a public utility and sets prices, this means an agent is interfering with the price and output that would exist if competitive forces were allowed to work.

During the third and fourth decades of the twentieth century, economists began to be increasingly aware of such deviations from the perfectly competitive market. The year 1933 is a landmark in the growth of interest in this subject, since two pioneering theoretical works—one by Joan Robinson and the other by Edward Chamberlain—appeared in this year.[4] Their work stimulated a number of other theoretical developments and many empirical studies of imperfect competition. This interest in imperfection also fed into a long-standing public concern with anti-trust policy.

Most economists who deal with patterns of imperfect competition study the influence of these market conditions on price and output. Economists are also concerned about resources wasted because of the inefficiency of productive enterprise under imperfect competition. From the perspective of economic sociology, however, it is important to note that theorists of imperfect competition are making new assumptions about the operation of political forces in the economy. Under perfect competition no firm has power. Under imperfect competition, by contrast, firms and other agents behave on certain occasions as *political agents*, sometimes even at the cost of economic gain. Consider the following examples: First, the very desire of a firm to control prices implies an interest in using political means to make the firm's market condition more comfortable. Second, firms sometimes set prices *not* directly on the basis of their own conditions of cost, but on the basis of political agreements with other firms. Third, firms sometimes behave uneconomically in the short run by cutting prices to expel competitors from the market so that they may enjoy a more satisfactory economic and political position in the long run. Fourth, firms sometimes set prices at a given level because the government has put pressure on them. Finally, firms sometimes *refuse* to combine because they fear po-

---

[4] Joan Robinson, *The Economics of Imperfect Competition* (London: Macmillan, 1933); Edward H. Chamberlain, *The Theory of Monopolistic Competition* (Cambridge: Harvard University Press, 1933).

litical and legal action on the part of a government interested in trust-busting. Analysis of all these examples associated with imperfect competition evidently requires definite assumptions about the nature of power relations in the economy; in fact the study of imperfect competition marks a formal wedding between economic and political analysis.

John Maynard Keynes

In considering the work of John Maynard Keynes (1883–1946) we shall stick to our political theme by sketching Keynes' ideas on the role of government in stabilizing the economy. Before doing so, however, we shall mention a few more general features of his work.

Keynes' work can be understood as an attempt to challenge and modify two features of classical economics. The first feature—and here Keynes modified more than challenged—concerned the conceptual level of economic analysis. In the classical tradition that had reached an apex in the work of Alfred Marshall (1842–1924), the focus of economics had been on the conditions of output and price for the *individual* firm. The condition of the economy as a whole—or as economists would say, the behavior of *aggregates*—was less problematical. Keynes insisted that aggregate economic conditions constituted an important focus for analysis. The second feature of classical economics that Keynes challenged was a long tradition beginning with the eighteenth-century writer, J. B. Say, and extending through the work of A. C. Pigou (1877–1959). Writers in this tradition assumed that in self-regulating economies resources are more or less fully and stably employed. Certain automatic adjustment mechanisms guarantee that changes in the level of capital and population will be absorbed smoothly, aside from minor periods of adjustment. Keynes maintained that in capitalist economies serious imbalances can develop and that long periods of unemployment and depression might be expected.

Keynes made his case by assembling a number of economic and non-economic variables. At the outset he maintained that an economy's level of income and employment can be viewed in two ways. First, from the standpoint of returns to individuals, a society's income is made up of that portion of returns that people spend for *consumption* plus that portion that they put aside as *savings*. Second, from the standpoint of production, income is made up of those goods destined for direct *consumption* by individuals and those goods destined to be used in *investment*—that is, in producing other goods and services. Looking at income in this double way, we obtain the following equation: Consumption + Savings = Consumption + Investment.

Having set up these definitions, Keynes made various assumptions about each of the ingredients—consumption, savings, and investment.[5] With regard to *consumption* and *savings*, Keynes maintained that consumers' tastes are fairly stable, and that in general consumers are not initiators in the economy. In addition, he assumed, as a "fundamental psychological law," that as a consumer's income rises he tends to lay aside an increasing proportion of his total income as savings. In the aggregate,

---

[5] The original statement of the Keynesian system is found in J. M. Keynes, *General Theory of Employment, Interest, and Money* (New York: Harcourt, Brace, 1936). A very clear secondary treatment is found in Alvin H. Hansen, *A Guide to Keynes* (New York: McGraw-Hill, 1953).

10

this means that a growth in the society's income is not accompanied by an equally great relative increase in consumption.

With regard to *investment*, Keynes also made a number of non-economic assumptions. Investment itself, he maintained, is a function of the rate of interest and the "marginal efficiency of capital." The latter term reflects businessmen's attitudes—in particular, an estimate they make concerning the profits to be expected from new investment. And in attempting to characterize these businessmen's attitudes, Keynes assumed simply that businessmen would predict that future returns would be approximately the same as present returns. The rate of interest is a function of the total stock of money (fixed by the monetary authority), and what Keynes called "liquidity preference." The latter term reflects certain attitudes of speculators, determining how they prefer to hold assets—as cash or securities.

Having set up these relations, Keynes then showed that under certain conditions the economy will experience unemployment, inflation, and various other instabilities. Notice that his reasoning rests on certain non-economic as well as economic assumptions. As Hansen summarizes it:

> Back of the consumption schedules is the psychological propensity to consume; back of the marginal efficiency schedule is the psychological expectation of future yields from capital assets; and back of the liquidity schedule is the psychological attitude to liquidity (expectations with respect to future interest rates). In addition to these . . . variables, rooted in behavior patterns and expectations, there is the quantity of money determined by the action of the Central Bank—an institutional behavior pattern.[6]

Finally, what sort of place did Keynes give the political dimension in his picture? His concern with political affairs appears primarily in his discussion of public policy. It is possible, Keynes and his followers argue, for the government to influence the level of national income and employment by manipulating its ingredients—consumption, savings, investment—and their determinants. Thus, in the role of *monetary policy*, the government manipulates the interest rate and the stock of money, influencing those variables that impinge on the marginal efficiency of capital and investment. By *fiscal policy* the government itself spends and invests, influencing both total consumption and investment. The major way in which the government does this is to build highways, public works, armaments, and so on. A related set of policies affects the *distribution of income*—taxation, welfare measures, subsidies, and the like. If such redistributional policies make for a more equal distribution of income (as graduated tax schedules would), this would increase consumption, because of the Keynesian principle that those with less absolute income will spend larger proportions of it.

Such governmental practices show that in the Keynesian system, as in many of the other bodies of economic thought we have examined, the strictly economic aspects of the system (income, price, consumption, investment) are intricately tied to political variables (taxation policy, defense policy, welfare policy, and so on). We cannot, in fact, especially in these days of big government, understand the workings of the economy without simultaneously knowing a great deal about public policy.

[6] *Op. cit.*, p. 166.

Conclusion

For the economic thinkers just examined, we may observe a kind of back-and-forth movement with respect to the relations between the economic and political dimensions. For the mercantilists the purposes of the economy and the polity are nearly indistinguishable; an increase of wealth means an increase of power, and power is to be used directly to increase wealth. Smith scrapped this notion of an undifferentiated economy and polity. The state and the economy, he argued, not only have different purposes but also should pursue these purposes as independently from one another as possible. For the economy, at least, its maximum growth will occur under conditions of free competition unfettered by political intervention.

Marx, while incorporating many features of classical economic thought into his own theory, revised the classical notions on the relations between the economic and political dimensions. In the sense that he saw the purposes of the economy and the polity as intimately associated, he looked back toward the mercantilists. He differed from them, however, insofar as he saw the polity as *subordinated* to economic considerations; furthermore, the role of the state was limited to buttressing the class relations that arose from the conditions of production. Keynes, again, saw more autonomy than Marx in the relations between polity and economy. For him the political authority can influence the condition of the economy. But he saw this influence operating not so much through the *direct* exercise of power as in the political manipulation of key economic variables and the unfolding of the economic consequences of these manipulations.

Sociological Aspects of Economic Life as Revealed in Sociological Thought

In considering the historical development of sociology, we again have to select only a few figures from a vast and complicated interplay of schools of social thought. In addition, we select a dimension that is political in part—the dimension concerning the integration of economic activities. Any division of labor—which leads people to pursue diverse and possibly conflicting lines of economic activity—may generate conditions of social strain. What social arrangements are geared to establishing peaceful, cooperative, and equitable interchange among economic agents? How does society attempt to control economic conflict? Sometimes the performance of the integrative function resides with the political authorities; at other times integration may be effected primarily by customs or codes that do not issue directly and immediately from the political authorities. In connection with the theme of integration we shall examine the thought of three men—Spencer, Durkheim, and Weber.

Herbert Spencer

For a number of decades in the late nineteenth and early twentieth centuries, Herbert Spencer (1820–1903) was perhaps the most influential figure in sociology. One reason for his great stature at that time is that his thought marked a confluence of two intellectual traditions—evolution and classical economics—both of which reached their apex in the last half of the nineteenth century.

From the evolutionary tradition, Spencer incorporated two funda-

12

mental notions—the society as an organism, and progressive social development. Spencer saw many similarities between the biological and social
organisms: Both are capable of growth; both increase in complexity of
structure as they grow in size; for both, this increasing complexity results
in the growth of highly specialized activities on the part of any given
structure; both display a close interdependence of parts; [7] for both, the life
of the whole organism is longer than the life of its parts. Although Spencer
himself stressed some differences between biological and social organisms,
and although organismic notions of society have been roundly attacked
since Spencer's time, this notion does at least have the virtue of depicting
society as a self-maintaining system of mutually interrelated parts (of which
economic activities are one set of parts).

Spencer viewed the process of social evolution as very similar to biological evolution. The social organism first undergoes an increase in integration; this may result from any number of causes but Spencer emphasized
expansion through warlike activities as a prime factor. A simple example
of increased integration would be the unification of two formerly separate
city-states into a single political entity. This increase in integration gives
rise to what Spencer calls a "dissipation of motion," which results in the
growth of increasingly differentiated (specialized) social structures. The unification of the city-states, for instance, gives rise to more complex and
specialized political activities to govern the new entity. Evolution as such
proceeds as an alternation between the forces of integration and the forces
of differentiation; the result is a process of growth *from* societies that are
homogeneous in structure *toward* those that are heterogeneous (with mi-
nute specializations in all social functions).

To give more concrete historical meaning to this general evolutionary
scheme, Spencer viewed all evolution in terms of two types of society—the
"military" and the "industrial." In the last analysis the former is integrated
by force. The military chief is its political head; industrial activitiy is
subordinated to military needs; the individual is subjugated to the state.
The principle of integration of the military society is *compulsory cooperation*; all integration (including the integration of economic activities)
stems from the actions of an undifferentiated politico-military authority.

The industrial society—toward which military societies evolve—contrasts with the military on all counts. Its political machinery is no longer
subordinated to the single military principle; differentiated democratic
structures, such as parliaments and cabinets, arise. Industrial activity
flourishes, independent of direct political control; in the economy, too,
differentiated processes of production, exchange, and distribution develop.
The individual is freed from the domination of the state. The principle of
integration of industrial societies, then, is *voluntary cooperation*; men enter
into relations with one another freely and contractually.

Spencer conceived the military and industrial types of society as
an abstract conceptual apparatus to account for the broad evolutionary
sweep of human history. He also saw the two types of society as opposed in
principle: "By as much as cooperation ceases to be compulsory, by so much
does it become voluntary; for if men act together they must do it either

---

[7] In Chapter 5 we shall organize our discussion of economic development around
the twin concepts of differentiation and integration, though our meaning of these terms
will differ somewhat from Spencer's.

willingly or unwillingly." [8] In the industrial society, the principle of integration is the principle of freedom; men interact by forming contractual agreements. Political intervention should be minimized, for it upsets the voluntarily coordinated activities of free individuals. Thus in the end Spencer viewed his industrial society much as Adam Smith did his competitive economy. Power is so differentiated and dispersed—and free men are so motivated—that integration is effected by balancing individual interests in a vast system of voluntary interchanges. Active social integration in the industrial society thus becomes unnecessary for Spencer, just as active political regulation becomes unnecessary for Smith.

Émile Durkheim

Most of the insights of Émile Durkheim (1858–1917) concerning economic integration are contained in his earliest major work, *The Division of Labor in Society*, published in 1893.[9]

Although Durkheim leveled a sharp attack at Spencer in *The Division of Labor*, his thought resembles Spencer's in certain respects. Durkheim was primarily interested in the ways in which social life is integrated. To conceptualize his position, he set up a dichotomy between two types of society—the segmental and the differentiated. What are the characteristics of these types, and how are they integrated?

The segmental society is a homogeneous society. The social division of labor is minimal, limited in the extreme case to that between the sexes and among persons of different ages. Durkheim compared his segmental society to the earthworm. It is composed of structurally-identical kinship units, which resemble the worm's rings; if some of these units are removed, they can be replaced immediately by the production of new and identical parts. In this way the segmental society differs from the complex society with qualitatively different role specializations—removal of some of which would leave the society without certain vital functions.[10] Durkheim insisted that the principle of homogeneity in segmental societies is based on the principle of kinship; therefore segmental societies are not identical to Spencer's military societies. Nevertheless, military and segmental societies do share the characteristic of structural homogeneity.

How are segmental societies integrated? Durkheim described this by the term "mechanical solidarity." Any disruptive act is met by a passionate and cruel reaction of vengeance by society against the offending party. This punishment reflects the collective values of the segmental society. These values, moreover, are more or less identical for all members; this identity follows from the basic homogeneity of segmental societies. The most striking instance of mechanical solidarity is found in repressive law (e.g., laws against rape, kidnapping, and murder, even in complex societies). Mechanical solidarity, then, consists of the subordination of the individual to the undifferentiated collective conscience of the society. There are resemblances between Durkheim's concept of mechanical solidarity and Spencer's concept of compulsory cooperation.

[8] Herbert Spencer, *The Principles of Sociology*, Vol. III (London: Williams and Norgate, 1897), p. 484.
[9] The English edition, translated by George Simpson, was published in 1933. The most recent edition is that published by The Free Press, Glencoe, Illinois, in 1949.
[10] See the discussion of the differences between segmentation and differentiation as types of social change, below, pp. 99–100.

14

Durkheim's view of the differentiated society also is similar to Spencer's notion of the industrial society. Both possess highly specialized role structures. Both encourage the emergence of individual differences, freed from the total domination of homogeneous segmental societies. The differences between their concepts of complex societies—and the nub of Durkheim's attack—involve how these societies are integrated.

Durkheim maintained that the only viable principle of integration permitted in Spencer's industrial society is the principle of contract or free exchange. No independent integrative action, above and beyond negative controls to prevent persons from hurting one another, is necessary. Durkheim doubted the possibility of stability in such a society, which would hang together only on the basis of momentary contacts among individuals. In contrast to Spencer, he maintained that powerful forms of integration operate in differentiated societies. Durkheim found this type of integration—which he termed "organic solidarity"—primarily in restitutive laws, which contain rules governing the conditions under which contractual relations can be considered valid. Other forms of organic solidarity above and beyond the law are customs, trade conventions, and implicit understandings among economic agents. Durkheim's difference with Spencer, then, is that he gave independent analytic significance to the problem of integration in complex societies.

Max Weber

In assessing the relations among types of societies and types of integration, both Spencer and Durkheim relied on simplified and abstract concepts—military society, segmental society, compulsory cooperation, organic solidarity, and so on. In the rich complexity of the empirical world such concepts are never manifested in pure form; each historical case is a mixture, showing relative dominance of one or more characteristics. The value in using such abstract constructs is to allow us to depict relations among variables in a precise, analytic manner.

Max Weber (1864–1920) refined this use of abstract concepts in his comparative analysis of social structure. In particular, he developed and used widely the notion of "ideal type." By this term he referred to a "one-sided accentuation . . . by the synthesis of a great many diffuse, discrete, more or less present and occasionally absent *concrete* individual phenomena, which are arranged [by the analyst] into a unified *analytical* construct. In its conceptual purity, this mental construct cannot be found anywhere in reality." [11] The analyst uses such ideal constructs to unravel and explain a variety of actual historical situations. Weber mentioned explicitly two kinds of ideal-type constructs—"historically unique configurations," such as "rational bourgeois capitalism"; and statements concerning historical evolution, such as the Marxist laws of capitalist development.[12]

One of Weber's enduring preoccupations was with the conditions under which industrial capitalism of the modern Western type would arise and flourish. Initially Weber was careful to distinguish industrial capitalism from other forms, such as finance capitalism and colonial capitalism. The former—sometimes called high capitalism or rational bourgeois capitalism—refers to the systematic and rational organization of *production* itself.

[11] Max Weber, *The Methodology of the Social Sciences* (Glencoe, Ill.: The Free Press, 1949), pp. 90, 93.
[12] *Ibid.*, pp. 93, 101–103.

The ideal-typical features of this kind of capitalism, according to Gerth and Mills' summary of Weber, are as follows:

> [The production establishment] is based on the organization of formally free labor and the fixed plant. The owner of the plant operates at his own risk and produces commodities for anonymous and competitive markets. His operations are usually controlled rationally by a constant balancing of costs and returns. All elements, including his own entrepreneurial services, are brought to book as items in the balance of his accounts.[13]

Weber was dealing with a much more detailed historical phenomenon than were Spencer and Durkheim, who spoke of whole classes of societies.

Having defined industrial capitalism, Weber sought to identify the historical conditions which give rise to it and which are most permissive for its continuing existence. One of his most famous arguments is that the rise of ascetic Protestantism, especially Calvinism, established social and psychological conditions conducive to this particular form of capitalism. Another well-known argument is that bureaucracy provides the most rational form of social organization for perpetuating industrial capitalism. We shall refer to both of these arguments later.[14] At present we shall remain with the theme of integration. What institutional structures are most permissive for industrial capitalism but at the same time regulate it?

Weber found many of these structures in the political-legal complex. Several property arrangements, for instance, are particularly advantageous for the existence of industrial capitalism: (a) Workers should not own their jobs, as they did (or almost did) under certain guild systems. This makes for sluggish labor turnover and for popular resistance to innovation. (b) Managers should not own their workers. Under conditions of slavery, for instance, managers are forced to allow slaves to have families, and they are unable to "lay off" slaves during slack seasons. From the standpoint of capitalist production, this is "irrational." (c) Workers should not own the means of production—tools, raw materials, and the like. This inhibits managers' ability to reallocate them as the occasion demands, and their ability to dicipline the workers. All ownership of the means of production should be in the hands of those who decide production matters. (d) Capitalists should not own or control opportunities for profit in the market. This introduces monopolistic rigidities into the exchange system.[15] What did Weber mean by these statements? Economists have long insisted on the importance of the mobility of resources in a capitalist economy. Weber was specifying some of the institutional conditions under which maximum mobility is both permitted and regulated.

Weber also stressed the political-legal regulation of money and exchange. Above all, rational capitalism cannot flourish unless the political authority guarantees the existence of a money supply with relatively stable values. As to the *type* of medium of exchange, Weber saw the advantage of the institutionalization of a generalized money currency (as opposed to payments in kind, which are limited to specific transactions),

[13] H. H. Gerth and C. Wright Mills (trans. and eds.), *From Max Weber* (New York: Oxford University Press, 1958), pp. 67–68.

[14] Below, pp. 41–42, 80.

[15] For full development of these themes, cf. Weber, *The Theory of Social and Economic Organization* (New York: Oxford University Press, 1947), pp. 228–278. See also pp. 40–49 of the Introduction to this volume by Talcott Parsons.

16

historical developments in economic sociology

since currency allows for expansion of the market and creation of credit. Finally, Weber, like Durkheim, stressed the importance of a legal framework to guarantee the validity of contracts, and advocated a functioning administrative and judicial system to enforce these legal regulations.

Weber never developed his economic sociology into a full theoretical system. Rather he remained at the level of generating historical insights about the pattern of institutional structures that surround important historical phenomena. Even so, it is possible to see his distinctive contribution to economic sociology. Unlike traditional economists, Weber was not interested in the regularities produced *within* the capitalist system of production (such as the business cycle), but in establishing the important background institutional conditions under which the capitalist system itself—and its regularities—could come into historical being.

Sociological Aspects of Economic Life as Revealed in Anthropological Thought

The figures we have treated in this chapter have focused on explaining economic activity in complicated civilizations (though Spencer and Durkheim, with their evolutionary emphasis, referred to homogeneous societies). In these civilizations we can observe structurally distinct economic forms (such as firms, banks, and markets) and records of distinct transactions (such as books of accounts, bank deposits, and price payments). The separate study of economic activities—and their relations to other activities—is facilitated in complex societies because these activities are highly visible. The anthropologist studying simple societies has no such advantage. Any activity he observes is likely to be indistinguishably and simultaneously economic, religious, political, and familial. This creates serious problems for the analytically separate study of economic life in these societies. Or, as Raymond Firth has put the problem,

> The principles of economics which are truly general or universal in their application are few. Most of those which purport to be general have been constructed primarily within the framework of ideas of an industrial, capitalist system. This means a machine technology, a monetary medium of exchange, an elaborate credit system using stocks and shares and banking institutions, developed private enterprise, and a social structure of an individualistic, Western kind. The anthropologist struggles with a diversity of types. Many are peasant systems, with money used for a limited range of transactions, a simple technology with hardly any machinery, and methods of enterprise, cooperation, credit, and income-getting very different from those in a Western economy. Some are truly primitive, with no monetary medium at all to facilitate the processes of exchange, distribution, and storage of wealth. The anthropologist's problem, then, is one of applying or translating economic principles in novel contexts. He is even deprived for the most part of the common means of measurement available to his economist colleague. Without money there is no simple means of reckoning prices. Even where money is used, its limited range inhibits easy measurement of the bulk of economic relations.[16]

In the past 40 years a number of anthropological investigations have shown that economic activities in simple societies are embedded in and guided by

[16] Raymond Firth, *Elements of Social Organization* (London: Watts, 1951), pp. 122–123.

principles of chieftainship, clanship, and kinship. These studies have concentrated mainly on production and exchange. Let us mention a few.

In 1922 Bronislaw Malinowski (1884–1942) published a pathbreaking study of economic activity among the native tribes of the Melanesian New Guinea archipelagoes.[17] In both production and exchange Malinowski saw kinship and chieftainship as critical in inducing individuals to undertake specific kinds of economic activity. In the production of a canoe, for instance, he discovered a distinctive division of labor among chief, experts, and helpers. But these individuals do not donate labor for specific and proportional wage payments; rather the aim of economic activity is "providing the chief or head man with the title of ownership of a canoe, and his whole community with its use." [18] In other spheres of production,

> Communal labour is . . . based upon the duties of . . . relatives-in-law. That is, a man's relatives-in-law have to assist him, whenever he needs their co-operation. In the case of a chief, there is an assistance on a grand scale, and whole villages will turn out. In the case of a commoner, only a few people will help. There is always a distribution of food after the work has been done, but this can hardly be considered as payment, for it is not proportional to the work each individual does.[19]

On the basis of these observations, Malinowski launched an attack on traditional Western views of economic motivation.

Malinowski also stressed the integrative significance of magic for economic activities. The construction of a canoe, again, is accompanied at every stage by magical rituals. Malinowski interpreted this magic as a kind of supplementary force to well-exercised craftsmanship, supplying "the psychological influence, which keeps people confident about the success of their labour, and provides them with a sort of natural leader." [20]

The impingement of non-economic variables appears even more clearly in the realm of exchange. Malinowski identified forms such as the pure gift, which usually involves presents (without expectation of return) between husband and wife, and between parents and children. Even forms of exchange that involve payment for services rendered are strictly regulated by custom. In still other cases material goods are traded for non-economic items such as privileges and titles.[21] As Malinowski repeatedly pointed out, conventional supply and demand theory cannot account for such patterns of exchange.

A few years after the appearance of Malinowski's monograph, Marcel Mauss (1872–1950), Durkheim's student and collaborator, produced a small volume entitled *The Gift*, in which he surveyed a vast anthropological literature on ceremonial exchange patterns.[22] In such exchanges Mauss observed binding obligations—on the giver to give, on the receiver to receive, and on the receiver to reciprocate (though the timing and exact amount of the return gift is open to much variation). Mauss, like Malinowski, found it impossible to interpret these traditional exchanges in purely

---

[17] Bronislaw Malinowski, *Argonauts of the Western Pacific* (London: Routledge, 1922).

[18] *Ibid.*, p. 158.

[19] *Ibid.*, p. 160.

[20] *Ibid.*, p. 116. For another monograph on the relations between magic and work, cf. Bronislaw Malinowski, *Coral Gardens and Their Magic* (London: Allen & Unwin, 1935).

[21] *Argonauts of the Western Pacific*, pp. 177–186.

[22] Marcel Mauss, *The Gift* (Glencoe, Ill.: The Free Press, 1954).

historical developments in economic sociology

utilitarian or economic terms. Rather he emphasized the gift as a symbolic binding-together of a kinship unit or tribe.[23] Moreover, Mauss stressed the "total" character of these primitive phenomena:

> These phenomena are at once legal, economic, religious, aesthetic . . . and so on. They are legal in that they concern individual and collective rights, organized and diffuse morality. . . . They are at once political and domestic, being of interest both to classes and to clans and families. They are religious; they concern true religion, animism, magic, and diffuse religious mentality. They are economic, for the notions of value, utility, interest, luxury, wealth, acquisition, accumulation, consumption and liberal and sumptuous expenditure are all present. . . . Moreover, these institutions have an important aesthetic side. . . . Nothing in our opinion is more urgent or promising than research into "total" social phenomena.[24]

The work of Firth also deserves mention, largely because it represents a more profound effort to *synthesize* anthropological research and economic theory. Malinowski, whose attitude toward technical economics was more negatively critical, fell short of this synthesis. In his monographs on the Maori of New Zealand and the Tikopia,[25] Firth organized his discussion around traditional economic categories of division of labor, income, capital, distribution and rational calculation; but he also showed how these activities were conditioned by the dynamics of chieftainship, kinship, magic, and prestige systems. In a more recent work on the economic structure of the Malay fishing industry,[26] Firth demonstrates how certain spheres of economic activity, especially marketing and credit, lend themselves to technical economic analysis, whereas other spheres, such as production and labor supply, are strongly influenced by familial, religious, and other non-economic variables.

Such anthropological researches suggest that the analysis of economic activity in undifferentiated and semi-differentiated societies requires a species of theory different from the highly developed technical economics suited to complex Western societies. In Chapter 4 we shall put forth some suggestions for the comparative analysis of such societies.

A Few Recent Trends in Economics and Sociology

Historically, economists, sociologists, and anthropologists have made various assumptions and assertions about the subject-matter of their neighboring fields. These assumptions and assertions, moreover, determine in part how they formulate generalizations and theories in their own fields. To conclude this chapter, we shall identify a few modern developments in economics and sociology that show at least an indirect concern with the overlap between the two fields.

Economics

1. Welfare economics. The life sciences (biology, bacteriology, and so on) concern the functioning of the organism, not as it

[23] *Ibid.*, pp. 70–71.
[24] *Ibid.*, pp. 76–78.
[25] Raymond Firth, *Economics of the New Zealand Maori*, rev. ed. (Wellington, New Zealand: Owen, 1959); *Primitive Polynesian Economy* (London: Routledge, 1939).
[26] *Malay Fishermen: Their Peasant Economy* (London: Kegan Paul, Trench, Trubner, 1946).

19

"ought to be" but as it "is." Medicine, on the other hand, is concerned with the "ought" of preserving and improving the health of the organism by applying the laws generated by the life sciences. Similarly, economics can be considered as the "value-free" study of the production, distribution, and exchange of scarce goods and services. But "welfare economics"—which has been a subject of some interest in recent decades—concerns the application of economic principles at the policy level to optimize the welfare of the individual and the community. Presumably, then, welfare economists should advise on tax policy, and so on, on the basis of economic principles.

In principle this program for welfare economics leads directly into the complex interaction of economic, political, religious, and other variables that appears in connection with practical social policy. In practice, however, welfare economists have not raised such issues. Many have taken an interest only in the effects on an individual's welfare that result from changes in his economic environment alone.[27] Many have been preoccupied with *potentially* relevant sociological questions: How is it possible to measure economic welfare? How is it possible to compare one individual's satisfaction with that of another? By what principle can we generalize from individual welfare states to the welfare of the community? [28] But welfare economists have seldom launched systematic empirical investigations of human preferences. Their policy principles are often rarefied. Consider, for instance, Pareto:

> Alternative [economic state] A has a higher group welfare than alternative B if and only if every member of the group is at least as well off, and if at least one person is better off, in A than in B. The opposite is true for B having a higher group welfare than A.[29]

Such a principle, while it may be logically consistent, still rests far from what we normally consider to be practical policy questions.

2. Organizational decision-making theory. As we shall see in Chapter 4, the neo-classical theory of the firm rests on several assumptions about goals, power, and knowledge. For analyzing a firm at any given time, its goals are assumed to be given and unchanging. The firm, moreover, neither controls its external environment (other firms, consumers) nor experiences internal political problems (such as conflict). Finally, classical theory is based on the assumption that the firm has full knowledge of its possible lines of behavior, and full knowledge of the consequences of each.

In any empirical situation these assumptions frequently break down. Businessmen in firms change their goals, they exercise power, and they lack knowledge. The theory of imperfect competition, as we saw, incorporated formally into economic theory those situations in which the firm controls output and prices. Modern organizational decision-making theorists have relaxed many of the remaining classical assumptions. They have identified situations in which firms (and other organizations) search for new information, change their goals, and experience internal conflict. Furthermore,

---

[27] This assumption is central to the welfare theory of Abram Bergson. See Jerome Rothenberg, *The Measurement of Social Welfare* (Englewood Cliffs, N. J.: Prentice-Hall, 1961), pp. 9–10.

[28] For a summary of the literature in modern welfare economics on these issues, cf. Kenneth E. Boulding, "Welfare Economics," in Bernard F. Haley (ed.), *A Survey of Contemporary Economics* (Homewood, Ill.: Irwin, 1952), pp. 5–12.

[29] Wording from Rothenberg, *op. cit.*, p. 62.

20

these theorists have brought a powerful new technique—computer simulation—to bear on the understanding and prediction of a firm's behavior.[30]

3. Game theory. In another way, the mathematical theory of games also modifies classical economic assumptions regarding goals, power, and knowledge. The game theorist sees two or more persons in interaction, each wishing to maximize gains or minimize losses. Furthermore, neither actor can fully predict the way in which the other is going to behave, nor is he able to control the other's behavior.

Using such assumptions, game theorists have created complicated models of behavior based on different strategies, different conditions of winning and losing, different conditions of competition and cooperation, and so on. The application of game theory to economics has been most noticeable in the fields of imperfect competition and labor relations.[31]

4. Economists have also turned to non-economic variables in labor economics, the economics of consumption, and the economics of growth. We shall mention these developments at various points in the later chapters.

Sociology

1. Industrial sociology. In the mid-1920's a number of experiments on productivity were conducted at the Hawthorne Works of the Western Electric Company in Chicago. Initially these experiments concerned the effects of lighting, rest periods, and so on, on work performance. During the course of the experiments, however, it became apparent to the investigators that these "physical" factors were not nearly so important in fostering high morale and productivity as various "human factors"—such as receiving status and being allowed to express grievances to a patient and responsive authority.[32]

Soon a "school" of thought developed—associated originally with Elton Mayo, T. North Whitehead, and Fritz J. Roethlisberger at Harvard. Known as the "human relations" approach because of its emphasis, this school came to be the core of the field of industrial sociology, which grew rapidly thereafter, with the establishment of centers at the University of Chicago, the Massachusetts Institute of Technology, and elsewhere. Industrial sociology has generated much research, commentary, and controversy in the past three decades. We shall refer to its findings later.

2. Various other sub-fields of sociology have contributed to the development of economic sociology in recent decades—the sociology of occupations, formal organizations, consumption, and stratification. Because these contributions are what the remainder of this book is about, we need only list them here.

---

[30] Recent summaries of organizational decision-making theory are found in R. M. Cyert and J. G. March, "A Behavioral Theory of Organizational Objectives," in Mason Haire (ed.), *Modern Organization Theory* (New York: Wiley, 1959), pp. 76–90; and March, "Some Recent Substantive and Methodological Developments in the Theory of Organizational Decision-Making," in Austin Ranney (ed.), *Essays on the Behavioral Study of Politics* (Urbana, Ill.: University of Illinois Press, 1962), pp. 191–208.

[31] The major work on the theory of games is John von Neumann and Oskar Morgenstern, *Theory of Games and Economic Behavior* (Princeton: Princeton University Press, 1944); also Martin Shubik, *Strategy and Market Structure* (New York: Wiley, 1959).

[32] The written material on the Western Electric researches is voluminous. A summary may be found in F. J. Roethlisberger, *Management and Morale* (Cambridge: Harvard University Press, 1950).

economics, sociology, and economic sociology

two

Two approaches are available to those who wish to compare disciplines. The first is *descriptive*. Thus economists may be described as spending their time in the study of why businessmen decide to produce the goods they do, how these goods are distributed through the market the way they are, and why people buy the kinds and amounts of goods they do. Political scientists study how legislatures and governmental bureaucracies work, why people vote the way they do, why parties campaign the way they do, and so on. In practice, sociologists study a sort of grab-bag of leftovers from these two disciplines. Although they do study some aspects of economic and social life, sociologists concentrate on prestige systems (social stratification and social classes), family life, urban life, race relations, experimental small groups, and so on. Furthermore, sociologists usually study large, complex societies. Anthropologists study many of the same things as sociologists but concentrate on small, simple societies and on kinship and religion—which seem to dominate these societies.

The second method of comparing disciplines is *analytic*. In this approach we ask several sets of questions:

1. What are the distinctive scientific problems that the field faces? What is it *about* economic life, family life, urban life, and so on, that is to be explained? Is it cyclical changes in the level of employment, changing rates of divorce, rates of migration to and from cities? Answers to such questions specify *dependent variables*—things to be explained.

2. What are the causes (or determinants, or factors, or conditions) of the behavior of the dependent variables? How do we go about explaining that which we wish to explain? Do changes in the rate of investment determine changes in level of employment? Or are changes in foreign trade more important? Does the fact that spouses are from different economic backgrounds make for a high probability of divorce? Or is religion more important? Answers to these questions specify the *independent variables*.

3. What are the *relations* governing the independent and dependent variables? One important set of relations concerns the problem of *classification* or *taxonomy*. On the one hand, what are the major types of results (dependent variables) to be expected? In studying family stability, for instance, is it enough to study divorced vs. non-divorced families alone? Or is it necessary to include legal separations, desertions without divorce, and other sub-types as well? On the other hand, what are the main types of operative factors (independent variables)? Is it enough to try to explain different divorce rates in terms of differences in religion and education of spouses, or is it necessary to add several psychological factors (for example, attitudes about sex) as causes of marital breakdown? A second set of relations involves the *logical ordering* of each set of variables. Is one independent variable (religion, for instance) more important than another (education, for instance) in accounting for different rates of divorce? Are all the independent variables conceived to rest at the same level of abstraction? Or do variables at one level (religious affiliation, for instance, at the social level) combine with variables at another level (sex attitudes, for instance, at the psychological level)? A third set of relations involves the ways in which the various independent and dependent variables are combined to generate testable *hypotheses* about the empirical world. An example of an hypothesis is: "Marriages with spouses from different religious backgrounds will show significantly higher rates of divorce than marriages with spouses with the same religious background." A systematically related group of such hypotheses is often referred to as an *explanatory model*.

To compare economics and sociology, we shall now proceed to an analytic characterization of each field. Although many distinctions can be made, some overlapping between the two fields still exists. Furthermore, the analytic distinctions we make are bound to be controversial. All who call themselves economists (econometricians, labor economists, institutional economists, some economic historians) do not agree about the precise nature of economics; all who call themselves sociologists (demographers, historians of social thought, small-group analysts, some social psychologists) are even more divided about their own field.

Economics as a Discipline

The following "informative introductory description" of economics appears in a well-known text on the subject:

> . . . the study of how men and society *choose*, with or without the use of money, to employ *scarce* productive resources to produce various commodities over time and distribute them for consumption, now and in the future, among people and groups in society.[1]

[1] Paul A. Samuelson, *Economics: An Introductory Analysis*, 5th ed. (New York: McGraw-Hill, 1961), p. 6.

From this definition let us build a statement of dependent variables, independent variables, and relations among these variables in economics.

Dependent Variables

A first set of dependent variables is found in the term "commodities." What is the level of the total production of goods and services in a society? What different kinds (shoes, guns, butter) are produced, and in what proportions? Economists thus attempt to account for variations in the level and composition of production.

A second set of dependent variables is found in the term "scarce productive resources." Goods and services are produced by the application of the following factors of production: (1) land, or the state of the natural resources, cultural values, and technical knowledge; (2) labor, or the level of motivation and skill of human beings; (3) capital, or the level of resources available for future production rather than immediate consumption; and sometimes (4) organization, or the principles of combination and recombination of the other factors. Organization involves the operation of institutions such as property and contract as well as the activity of entrepreneurs. Economists are thus interested in explaining the levels and relative proportions of these resources in productive use, and the techniques by which they are combined.

A third set of dependent variables is indicated by the term "distribute." Which individuals and groups receive the goods and services generated in the productive process? Or, to put it in terms of payments, what is the distribution of income generated in the economic process?

The basic dependent variables in economics, then, are production, techniques of organizing resources, and distribution of wealth. In the Keynesian system, the basic dependent variables are the volume of employment (or the proportion of available labor in productive use at any given time) and the national income (or the total level of production).[2] Even in small sub-fields of economics the specific problems posed turn out to be instances of the basic dependent variables. In the study of wages in labor economics, for instance, the following elements generally need explaining:

> (a) the general level of wages in the nation and its movements during past decades, (b) the wage spread between occupations and changes in the spread from time to time, (c) wage differentials between regions and areas and alterations in such differentials over the course of time, (d) inter-industry differentials and shifts in them, (e) inter-firm differentials in a locality and changes therein, and (f) differentials between persons working in the same occupation within a plant.[3]

Independent Variables

How are the level and composition of production, the allocation of resources, and the distribution of wealth determined? In the broad comparative sweep these may be determined by political regulation, custom, religious decree, and so on. Formal economic analysis, however, has traditionally stressed supply and demand in the market as the

---

[2] *The General Theory of Employment, Interest and Money* (New York: Harcourt, Brace, 1936), p. 245.
[3] Richard A. Lester, *Labor and Industrial Relations: A General Analysis* (New York: Macmillan, 1951), p. 53.

economics, sociology, and economic sociology

immediate independent variables. For any given commodity—e.g., shoes—a person will be willing to buy much if it costs little, little if it costs much. The producer of this commodity will be willing to supply much if the price is high, little if the price is low. The price of the commodity falls at that point where the demand curve and the supply curve intersect.

This supply-demand principle is used to account for the behavior of all the dependent variables. The level and composition of production depend on the existing supply and demand conditions for products; the level and composition of the factors of production depend on the same kinds of conditions for them; and finally, the proportions of income received by different individuals and groups depend on the supply and demand conditions governing the relations among economic agents.

Relations among Variables

One of the most famous models in economics concerns the prediction of the quantity of a given commodity that an individual firm will produce under conditions of perfect competition. Given a certain level of demand, the firm can expect to receive a given price (revenue) for each item it produces. But the firm itself has to pay for the factors it utilizes in production. These costs determine the conditions of supplying its commodity to consumers. By a series of constructions, economists have built a model that predicts that the firm will produce that quantity of a commodity at which the *cost* of producing the extra unit of the commodity (marginal cost) equals the *revenue* that it will receive for that extra unit (marginal revenue). Basically, this model says that the value of the dependent variable (quantity of the commodity produced by a firm) is a function of the value of two sets of independent variables (demand and supply).

Turning to the analysis of aggregates, the Keynesian model identifies the independent variables—in the first instance—as the propensity to consume, the schedule of the marginal efficiency of capital, and the rate of interest.[4] The propensity to consume is a demand category; the marginal efficiency of capital rests on expectations about profits to be returned for investments; and the rate of interest rests on the supply of money and the demand for liquidity. By manipulating the values of these independent variables, Keynes established a set of predictions leading to unemployment of a society's resources and reduction of its national product (dependent variables). This is the essence of the Keynesian equilibrium model.

The Importance of "Givens" in Economic Analysis

In these illustrative economic models the behavior of various dependent variables—prices, level of production, etc.—rests on the operation of the economic forces of supply and demand. But in the real world things are not so simple. Many dozens of variables—economic, political, legal, religious—affect prices and production, and if a complete picture of economic life were to be given, many of these kinds of variables would have to be incorporated into economic models. How do economists deal with this empirical complexity? A common method is to realize that while non-

---

[4] *Op. cit.*, p. 245. Above, pp. 10–12, for a definition of these variables and a statement of the relations between these variables and the other Keynesian variables.

economics, sociology, and economic sociology

economic variables affect supply and demand conditions, it is necessary *for purposes of analysis* to assume that these variables do not change. This is the meaning of Samuelson's statement that economic analysis takes institutions and tastes as given; [5] by "given" he means that potential sources of variation are assumed not to vary.

To illustrate: In constructing his equilibrium system, Keynes considered several things as given: the existing skill of the labor force, the existing equipment, the existing technology, the existing degree of competition, the existing tastes of the consumer, the existing attitudes of people toward work, and the existing social structure.[6] All these, if they varied, would affect the independent variables (e.g., the propensity to consume and the marginal efficiency of capital) and through them the dependent variables (employment and national income); but they are assumed not to vary.

Similarly, in wage analysis, a whole array of economic and non-economic variables affects wage differentials:

> Varying rates of population growth are an important factor in geographic differentials. Industrial differentials are to be explained, in large measure, by the nature of the industry . . . and by the policies and bargaining strength of the union or unions with jurisdiction in the industry. Inter-plant differentials locally for the same type and grade of labor seem to be the result mainly of four factors: industry differentials, differences in management and plant efficiency, differences in employer wage policies, and the combination of company hiring policies and worker job behavior. Custom is also important.[7]

For any specific model of wage differentials, however, only a few of these factors are incorporated; the others are either unimportant or unvarying.

One of the most important "givens" in traditional economic analysis is that of economic rationality: If an individual is presented with a situation of choice in an economic setting, he will behave so as to maximize his economic position.[8] If this "given" is presented as a simple empirical generalization, it is unsatisfactory in many instances, for people often behave uneconomically. As an investigative device, however, "economic rationality" allows the economist to proceed *as if* the only independent variables were measurable changes in price and income. His world thus simplified, the economist is enabled to create elegant theoretical solutions to economic problems. Economic analysis thus faces a dilemma: to create theoretically advanced models while oversimplifying the non-economic world or to take account of the complexity of the non-economic world while sacrificing theoretical generality.

Sociology as a Discipline

In sociology the task of specifying variables and relations is more difficult than in economics. Widespread disagreement

[5] *Op. cit.*, 2nd ed., 1951, p. 15.

[6] *Op. cit.*, p. 245.

[7] Lester, *op. cit.*, p. 68.

[8] This postulate has had many intellectual variations and refinements in the history of economic thought. In classical economics up to about the 1870's (especially in the thought of Ricardo and Mill), the postulate took the form of an application of the utilitarian principle of hedonistic calculus; in the several decades thereafter the utility theory of Jevons and others came to predominate; and in modern times indifference curve analysts have attempted to iron out some of the difficulties of the earlier versions.

economics, sociology, and economic sociology

among sociologists about the fundamental problems and concepts of their discipline has led to a mushrooming of variables. Because of this superabundance, sociological analysts are unable to present simple and coherent models; instead, analysis often focuses on categorizing social facts. Necessarily, then, our analytic characterization of sociology will have to be approximate. It will omit several subdivisions of sociology (especially demography and social psychology), and it will gloss over many disagreements concerning fundamental features of the field.

Dependent Variables

Sociological analysis begins with a problem. Posing a problem means identifying some variation in human behavior and framing a "why" question about this variation. Such variation becomes the dependent variable—that which is to be explained. The variation may involve a single event (Why did violence erupt in the Congo when it did?); it may involve presumed regularities in the occurrence of events (Why are colonial societies emerging from domination prone to outbursts of hostility?); or, at a higher level, it may involve questions of structural variation in large classes of events (Why do feudal land patterns arise and persist? Why do they break down, sometimes in different ways?).

After isolating a certain problem, the investigator must specify concrete units that identify the dependent variable.[9] These concrete units are found in the *units of social structure* and in *variations of human behavior oriented to social structure.*

"Social structure" is a concept used to characterize recurrent and regularized interaction among two or more persons. The basic units of social structure are not persons as such, but selected aspects of interaction among persons, such as roles (e.g., businessman, husband, church-member) and social organization, which refers to structured clusters of roles (e.g., a bureaucracy, a clique, a family). Social organization refers to more than goal-oriented collectivities (e.g., business firms, hospitals, government agencies); it may refer to informal organizations (such as gangs or neighborhood friendship groups) and diffuse collectivities (such as ethnic groupings). The important defining features of social structure are that interaction is selective, regularized, and regulated by various social controls.

In the analysis of social structures, three basic concepts are particularly important: (1) *Values* refer to beliefs that legitimize the existence and importance of specific social structures and the kinds of behavior that transpire in social structure. The value of "free enterprise," for instance, endorses the existence of business firms organized around the institution of private property and engaged in the pursuit of private profit. (2) *Norms* refer to standards of conduct that regulate the interaction among individuals in social structures. The norms of contract and property law, for instance, set up obligations and prohibitions on the agents in economic transactions. As the examples show, at any given level of analysis norms are more specific than values in their control of interaction in social structures. (3) *Sanctions*—including both rewards and deprivations—refer to the use of various social resources to control the behavior of personnel in social structures. Aspects of this control include the establishment of roles, the

---

[9] In practice the operation of posing problems and the operation of specifying concrete units proceed simultaneously and interact with one another.

inducement of individuals to assume and perform roles, and the control of deviance from expected role performance. Examples of sanctions are coercion, ridicule, appeal to duty, withdrawal of communication, and so on.

A concept which unifies the elements of social structure—including roles, collectivities, values, norms, sanctions—is the concept of *institutionalization*. This refers to distinctive, enduring expectations whereby these elements are combined into a single complex. When we speak of the institutionalization of American business, for instance, we refer to a more or less enduring pattern of roles and collectivities (e.g., businessmen and firms), values (e.g., free enterprise), norms (laws of contract and property, informal business codes), and sanctions (profits, and so on).

Many dependent variables in sociology are stated as follows: Why are the elements of social structure patterned the way they are? Another class of dependent variables is specified in terms of systematic variations in human behavior oriented to social structure. Given some structure, when can conformity be expected? What are the consequences of conformity for the social structure? When can deviance from structured behavior be expected? What are the different forms of deviance, and why does one type of deviance rather than another arise? What are the consequences for the social structure of different kinds of deviance? Specifying the possible "consequences" of conformity or deviance involves identifying a further range of dependent variables—reactions to deviance (social control), changes in social structure, persistence of structural patterns, collective outbursts.

What are the major types of social structure? This question is usually answered by turning to some notion of the basic functions, or directional tendencies, of social systems. These functions concern the general orientations of social life. Or as the question is often put: What are the exigencies that must be met in order for the social system to continue functioning? Analysts who attempt to identify the basic directional tendencies of social systems speak of "functional exigencies." Typical exigencies include:

1. Modes of creating and maintaining the cultural values of a system. For some systems, such as societies, this involves long periods of socialization and complex structures such as families, churches, and schools.

2. Modes of producing, allocating, and consuming scarce goods and services (sometimes called the economic function). Typical structures that specialize in this function are firms, banks, and other agencies of credit.

3. Modes of creating, maintaining, and implementing norms governing interaction among units in the system (sometimes called the integrative function), such as the law and its enforcement agencies.

4. Coordinating and controlling the collective actions of the system or a collectivity within it, usually by the state (the political function).

The usual basis for classifying social structures is to indicate the basic functions they serve—political, economic, familial, religious, educational. The classification of social structures in this way involves assigning *primacy* of function only. Even though "religious structure" is a concept applied to a clustering of rites or an organized church, the social significance of this bundle of activities is not exhausted by this concept. Analytically, the concrete religious structure has a "political aspect," an "economic aspect," and so on. The notion of structure, then, is used to identify theoretically significant properties of concrete clusters of activities devoted primarily but not exclusively to meeting some social exigency.

Notice the overlap between sociology and economics in the para-

economics, sociology, and economic sociology

graphs above. One of the functions considered essential in sociological analysis concerns economic life, the focus of economic analysis itself. At this point economic and sociological analysis overlap. Despite this common subject-matter, the basic dependent variables in each field differ. Economics is concerned especially with variations in the level of production, techniques of production, and distribution of goods and services; sociology is concerned with variations in social structure (including values, norms, sanctions) and variations in behavior oriented to this structure.

Independent Variables

The sociological concepts listed thus far—*viz.*, those revolving around the notion of social structure—are used mainly to identify dependent variables. They do not provide hypotheses about processes of social adjustment, maladjustment, and change; they do not themselves constitute explanations. To generate these additional ingredients of sociological analysis one must take account of several classes of independent variables. Among the most important of these are the concepts of strain, reactions to strain, and attempts to control reactions to strain.

1. Strain. Social systems are never perfectly integrated. The sources of malintegration, moreover, may arise from outside or inside the system. An example of externally imposed strain is economic shortages arising from a blockade of shipping by a foreign power during periods of international hostility. An example of internally generated strain is the build-up of "contradictions" such as those envisioned by Marx in his model of capital accumulation. The general presumption underlying the concept of "strain" is that it imposes integrative problems on the system and subsequently causes adjustments, a new form of integration, or a breakdown.

Among the many types of strain arising in social systems, the following are common: (1) Ambiguity in role expectations, in which information regarding expectations is unclear or lacking altogether. Many cite the case of the modern American woman, whose traditional domestic role has become uncertain, as a typical example of role ambiguity. (2) Conflict among roles, in which role expectations call for incompatible types of behavior. An example is the Negro doctor, whose occupational role calls for deference from others, but whose racial role traditionally calls for deference to others. (3) Discrepancies between expectations and actual social situations. An example of this is an unemployment level of 15 per cent in a society committed to high levels of employment. (4) Conflicts of values in a system. These may result, for instance, from the rapid migration of large numbers of ethnically alien persons into a society.

2. Reactions to strain. The initial reactions to situations of strain tend to be disturbed reactions which are frequently (but not always) deviant and malintegrative from the standpoint of the social system. Though the number and types of deviance have never been catalogued fully, a variety of specific social problems arise from deviance: crime, alcoholism, hoboism, suicide, addiction, mental disorders, outbursts of violence, and social movements. Each, while it involves the operations of psychological variables, is social insofar as it affects the structure and functioning of social systems.

3. Attempts to control reactions to strain. Given some strain and some threat of deviant behavior, two lines of attack are available at the social level to reduce the possibly disruptive consequences. (1) Structuring the social situation so as to minimize strain. Examples are the institutionalization of

priorities (so that conflicting expectations are ranked in a hierarchy of importance for the actor); scheduling activities (so that demands that would conflict if made simultaneously may be worked out serially); shielding evasive activity (so that illegitimate behavior is permitted so long as it does not openly disrupt the legitimately structured role-expectations); the growth of ideologies that justify certain types of deviance as "exceptions" while reaffirming, dominant norms of the situation, perhaps by paying lip service to them. (2) Attempting to control reactions to strain once they have arisen. This involves the application of sanctions by various agencies of social control, such as the police, the courts, etc.

These items are some of the major independent variables that help us account for the persistence and change of behavior oriented to social structures. To label strain, reactions to strain, and attempts to control these reactions as independent variables only oversimplifies the field of sociology. The investigator who is interested in explaining juvenile delinquency (reaction to strain) is, of course, treating it as a dependent variable. If, however, we start with the notion of social structure and related concepts, it is possible to see the sense in which the concepts just discussed are to be treated as independent. A full account of the relations among the major sociological concepts would include discussions of many feedback processes and mutual interdependencies among variables. A reorganization of social structure, for instance, frequently sets up strains, which in turn initiate new processes of deviance and social control. Our own division of the field into dependent and independent variables is the result of taking the elements of social structure as our starting point for exposition.

Relations among Variables in Sociology

Much of sociological analysis still involves classifications that organize facts. Despite the shortage of full-scale explanatory models in sociology, we can isolate two types:

1. Process models. These refer to changes of variables *within* a given social structure. These changes result from the performance of roles, or the re-establishment of equilibrium by the operation of social controls in the face of strain. Process models are used in analyzing rates of social mobility and certain types of social control (for instance, psychotherapy, which often "rehabilitates" persons considered to be "disturbed"). In these examples the social structure is unchanged.

2. Change models. Attempts to control strain and restore the social system to equilibrium sometimes fail, giving rise to a new type of equilibrium. The movement to a new equilibrium may be *controlled* (e.g., when a new law is passed by the constituted authorities to meet a pressing social problem) or *uncontrolled* (e.g., when a revolutionary party overthrows the authority and sets up a new constitution and government). The new equilibrium, moreover, may be precarious; changes may necessitate further change. Repeated failure of social control mechanisms may result in the disintegration of the system. All involve changes in the social structure.

The Problem of "Givens" in Sociological Analysis

Systematic analysis of social systems assumes that biological, psychological, and cultural variables are constant. Every sociological statement, however, implies a certain unvarying assumption about

economics, sociology, and economic sociology

human nature. For example, to assert that role ambiguity is a source of strain in social systems is to assume that ambiguity gives rise to anxiety that drives men to react against strain. Such psychological "postulates"—always open to empirical doubt—are far from uniformly accepted in sociology; certainly the field does not display the conspicuous continuity that economics does with the postulate of economic rationality.

Research Methods
in Economics and Sociology

The most rigorous form of investigation in social scientific analysis is the *experimental method*—to create two situations (one experimental and one control) that are alike in all respects except for one presumed causal factor, then to vary this factor in the experimental situation and compare the outcome with the control situation, in which the factor is not varied. With the exception of small-group analysis, this method is seldom used either in economics or in sociology.

One alternative to the experimental method is the *statistical method,* by which certain factors are held constant or canceled out by statistical manipulation. For example, suppose we wish to trace the long-term trend of potato prices over years. We know that potato prices vary seasonally as well as year by year, but we do not wish to measure the seasonal variation. So we calculate the average seasonal variation for all the fifty years, and cancel out seasonal fluctuations for each individual year by adding or subtracting the average seasonal variation from the actual prices. In this way we come closer to removing the seasonal fluctuations, and thus get a truer picture of uncontaminated long-term price trends, which we may then relate to other variables. This sort of statistical analysis, as well as various tests of association (such as regression analysis) receives wide application both in economics and in sociology.

Another alternative to the experimental method is the *comparative method,* frequently used when the number of cases is too small to permit statistical manipulation. A classic example of the comparative method in sociology is found in Max Weber's studies on religion.[10] Given that certain societies had developed rational bourgeois capitalism, Weber asked what characteristics these societies had in common. Then, turning to societies that had not developed this kind of economic organization (e.g., India, China), he asked in what respects they differed from the former societies. In this way he attempted to demonstrate that the religious factor accounted for the differences. This kind of comparative method is employed widely in sociology; in economics it is used mainly by economic historians and those interested in the development of the emerging nations.

Mathematical models are used much more frequently in economics than in sociology. Economics is more productive of neat, simple models that lend themselves to mathematical formulation; and it deals with data (prices, income, etc.) that are either pre-quantified or much more readily quantifiable than many sociological data. In sociology mathematical models are sometimes employed in the analysis of population and small groups, and occasionally in the analysis of voting behavior and social mobility.

The *case study* method is used in both economics and sociology. An example from economics is the studies of patterns of imperfect competition

[10] Below, pp. 40–41.

in particular industries; an example from sociology is the studies of patterns of social class behavior in a local community. In particular, industrial sociology has shown a proclivity to approach industrial work situations predominantly by using the "case" or "clinical" method.[11]

In both economics and sociology some data simply "appear" for social investigators in the normal course of social events and are "there," ready to be analyzed. Examples of such data are the stock market prices published in daily newspapers, unemployment figures collected by government agencies, and the social statistics presented in census reports. In other cases, investigators must gather their own data, usually by the *survey method*—i.e., a sample of a population with the desired data is interviewed. In economics the survey method is used widely to collect facts about households and firms—their assets and expenditures, their attitudes about future states of the market, their plans to purchase, their intentions to invest, reasons for investing, attitudes toward the interest rate, and so on.[12] In sociology the survey method is even more widely used, mainly to assess attitudes and opinions (for example, preferences for political candidates, attitudes about teenage dating, and so on). The attitudinal data produced by surveys supplement the recorded statistics, though the attitudes gleaned in casual interview situations often are "superficial."

The Analytic Focus
of Economic Sociology

Economic sociology is *the application of the general frame of reference, variables, and explanatory models of sociology to that complex of activities concerned with the production, distribution, exchange, and consumption of scarce goods and services.*[13]

The first focus of economic sociology is on economic activities alone. The economic sociologist asks how these activities are structured into roles and collectivities,[14] by what values they are legitimized, by what norms and sanctions they are regulated, and how these sociological variables interact.

The second focus of economic sociology is on the relations between sociological variables as they manifest themselves in the economic context and sociological variables as they manifest themselves in non-economic contexts. How, for instance, do familial roles articulate with occupational role of a local community and the control of its political structure? This relational focus includes both situations in which economic and non-economic structures are integrated with one another and situations in which the two

[11] George C. Homans, "The Strategy of Industrial Sociology," *American Journal of Sociology* (1948–1949), 54:331–334; Wilbert E. Moore, "Current Issues in Industrial Sociology," *American Sociological Review* (1947), 12: 651–652.

[12] For assessments of some of the problems of using the survey method in economics, see George Katona, "The Function of Survey Research in Economics," in Mirra Komarovsky (ed.), *Common Frontiers of the Social Sciences* (Glencoe, Ill.: The Free Press and the Falcon's Wing Press, 1957), pp. 358–371; and Katona and Eva Mueller, *Consumer Expectations, 1953-1956* (Ann Arbor: Survey Research Center, Institute for Social Research, University of Michigan, n.d.), pp. 7–11.

[13] Compare this definition with Wilbert Moore's definition of industrial sociology (which is one branch of economic sociology): "The field of industrial sociology . . . is concerned with the application or development of principles of sociology relevant to the industrial mode of production and the industrial way of life." "Industrial Sociology: Status and Prospects," *American Sociological Review* (1948), 13: 383.

[14] This emphasis in economic sociology is very close to that tradition of economics concerned with the division of labor.

economics, sociology, and economic sociology

structures operate at cross-purposes. In the latter situations we shall expect to find many strains, reactions to strain, and attempts to control these reactions. From this interplay of conflicting forces we shall also expect to observe various outcomes, such as re-equilibration and deviance.

This interplay of sociological variables in the economic and non-economic spheres can be observed in two settings: (1) *Within* concrete economic units. In the industrial firm, for instance, the economic sociologist studies the status systems, power and authority relations, deviance, cliques and coalitions, and the relations among these phenomena. This intra-unit focus is emphasized in that branch of economic sociology called industrial sociology. (2) *Between* economic units and their social environment. At one level the economic sociologist studies the relations between economic interests and other interests (legal, political, familial, religious) in both the community and the larger society. At a higher level he studies the relations between the economy considered as an analytic system of society and the other systems. This inter-unit focus leads to the "larger issues" of economic sociology—e.g., public policy, labor-management conflict, and relations between economic classes—that lie in the tradition of Marxian and Weberian thought. Finally, the economic sociologist studies the distinctively sociological aspects of the central economic variables themselves—money as one of many types of sanctions in social life.

Subdivisions of Economic Sociology

Many subdivisions of sociology can be conceived as proper parts of economic sociology. Among these are occupational sociology, the sociology of work, the sociology of complex organizations (at least that part which deals with economic bureaucracies), industrial sociology, plant sociology, the sociology of consumption, and so on.[15]

Relations between Economic Sociology and Economics

Even though economic sociology and economics deal with the same complex of activities, there is little *formal* overlap between them because each field operates with different classes of dependent variables, independent variables, and explanatory models. But this is not the whole story. The *empirical* interdependence of economic and sociological variables is omnipresent. Consider the following: (1) Persistent tinkering with wage levels (economic variable) on the part of management is likely to give rise to political changes inside and outside the plant. Inside it may strengthen cliques of workmen and heighten their propensity to subvert management's authority. Outside the plant it may foster the formation of a labor union or excite activity on the part of an existing one. (2) These informal work cliques and labor unions may then engage in political activities which give rise to economic changes. In a spirit of defiance, cliques of workmen may slow their work rate and thus depress the level of output of the firm. The labor union may challenge management, effecting perhaps a new wage level.

[15] For various attempts to specify such subdivisions, cf. Clark Kerr and Lloyd H. Fisher, "Plant Sociology: The Elite and the Aborigines," in Komarovsky (ed.), *op. cit.*, pp. 284–286; Edward Gross, *Work and Society* (New York: Crowell, 1958), p. 45; Delbert C. Miller and William H. Form, *Industrial Sociology* (New York: Harper, 1951), pp. 14–23.

Relations between
Economic Sociology and Psychology

The Postulate of Rationality Again

An enduring feature of economics is the postulate of a rational economic man. Because men are ignorant of their environment, because they make mistakes, because they live by habit and rule of thumb—this postulate is inadequate. Moreover, because the social world is characterized by the *interplay* of so many non-economic and economic variables, no one set of variables will completely dominate in any social setting.

Should we then abandon the notion of economic rationality? Perhaps not; at least four meanings of economic rationality are current, and *some are more acceptable than others.*

1. The least acceptable meaning of economic rationality is the argument that, as a matter of psychological fact, material satisfactions are the sole motivating factor in man's existence, and that he chooses rationally only among these material satisfactions. This version has been discredited.

2. If it is argued that although economic rationality may not be *the* total psychology of man but that behaviorally man acts rationally when faced with economic situations, the notion becomes more acceptable. Although men in all societies "economize," the number and kinds of situation in which men economize are extremely variable. For example, people in a simple society might display calculation in allocating resources to produce agricultural goods; but in exchanging these goods they might rely on highly traditionalized, "uneconomical" gift-giving to kinsmen and tribesmen.

3. If an analyst uses the notion of economic rationality merely as an investigational device for conceptual simplification, he presents a strong argument in its favor. He advances no particular psychological theories or existential claims, but uses the notion to manage the enormous motivational variability of his empirical world. Economic rationality then becomes merely a provisional set of assumptions. In treating rationality in this way, of course, the analyst should also assume that his conceptual simplification is subject to revision or rejection if it seems unhelpful in analyzing the scientific problems he faces.

4. A final way of treating economic rationality is to consider it as an institutionalized value. Rationality now becomes something more than a psychological postulate; it may be a standard of behavior to which people conform or from which they deviate. Thus in the American business firm it is not only the businessman's personal desire for profits but also the threat of negative social sanctions (e.g., ridicule or loss of position) that makes him follow the criteria of efficiency and cost-reduction. The economic sociologist must retain this social meaning of economic rationality, for it lies at the heart of one of his central variables—social control.

Psychological Research
and Economic Sociology

In general, economic sociology studies the relations between variables such as market conditions and purchases, strains and the formation of new social groups. Many of these variables lie at the social and behavioral levels. To connect these variables certain intervening

economics, sociology, and economic sociology

psychological states must be postulated. Consider the following examples.

1. The psychological states of "morale" and "satisfaction" of workers depend in large part on the social conditions of the work place, such as the method of supervision, the level of worker participation in decisions, level of interaction with other workers, and so on.[16] These psychological states in turn determine many kinds of worker response, such as absenteeism, accidents, pace of work, and industrial conflict. In this way "morale" intervenes between social variables and behavioral outcomes. Social psychologists (and some persons who call themselves industrial sociologists as well) are interested in states like morale as subjects in themselves—i.e., as dependent variables.[17] But from the standpoint of economic sociology as formally defined, they are intervening variables.

2. The psychological states of "attitudes" intervene in similar ways. For instance, if the major focus of psychological reference of wage workers at one skill level is workers at the next higher level, they will behave differently in the face of a wage increase for the higher-level workers than if their focus of reference were the absolute level of their own wages.[18] Attitudes also assume significance as determinants at different phases of business cycles and financial crises.[19]

A final point of articulation between psychology and economic sociology concerns the motivational patterns of persons who enter a particular occupational role. These distinctive motivations are relevant both for predicting who will be recruited into these roles and for understanding how these recruits will respond to social situations once they assume the roles.[20]

Conclusion

In this chapter we have established analytically what economic sociology is about. This required a preliminary excursion into the nature of economics and sociology. We also set off economic sociology from psychology. In the remainder of the volume we shall observe how the general variables of economic sociology work out in particular empirical settings. We begin in Chapter 3 with relations between the economic sub-system of society and its other major sub-systems.

---

[16] Below, pp. 82–86.

[17] For a brief summary of research work on morale and motivation in industry, see Daniel Katz, "Morale and Motivation in Industry," in Wayne Dennis, et al., *Current Trends in Industrial Psychology* (Pittsburgh: University of Pittsburgh Press, 1949), pp. 145–170.

[18] For an exploration of the importance of reference-groups in studying economic phenomena, see Seymour Martin Lipset and Martin Trow, "Reference Group Theory and Trade Union Wage Policy," in Komarovsky (ed.), *op. cit.*, pp. 391–411.

[19] George Katona and Lawrence R. Klein, "Psychological Data in Business Cycle Research," *American Journal of Economics and Sociology* (1951–1953), 12: 11–13.

[20] William E. Henry, "The Business Executive: The Psychodynamics of Social Role," *American Journal of Sociology* (1948–1949), 54: 286–291.

the economy
and other social
sub-systems

three

In assessing the research relevant to economic sociology, we shall proceed first on a grand scale, then on a small scale, then on a grand scale again. In this chapter we shall attack the subject at the *societal* level. We shall divide society tentatively into a number of sub-systems—one of which is the economy—and show the operation of economic and non-economic variables in the interaction among these sub-systems. In Chapter 4 we shall continue to focus on the general variables of economic sociology, but as they manifest themselves in detailed *economic processes*—specifically, production, exchange, and consumption. Finally, in Chapter 5, we shall return to the societal level, and observe the interaction among economic and non-economic variables in processes of *structural change* associated with economic and social development.

The Concept
of System and Sub-system

In the last chapter we defined the concept of structure as the recurrent and regularized interaction among two or more persons. This interaction is regulated by values, norms, and sanctions. Social structures are classified in terms of some set of basic directional tendencies of social systems in general. We tentatively identified several such tendencies—the creation, maintenance, and transmission of cultural values; the pursuit of economic activity; the conduct of political activity, and the maintenance of social integration.

Now we introduce a concept at a higher level of abstraction than social structure—the concept of social system. This refers to the patterning of structural units in such a way that changes in one or more units set up pressures for adjustment (or other types of change) on the part of other units. The Marxian view of society constitutes one type of system, since changes in the economic structure (for instance, the introduction of the capitalist mode of production) bring about adjustments of the political structure so that political agencies buttress the class relations arising from these economic arrangements. Other views of social systems allow for a greater degree of mutual influence among the component structures. In any case, the notion of system is an analytic concept that enables us to talk about the relations among structural units in sociology and to generate propositions about these relations.

How do we classify systems? At the societal level we refer to the same directional tendencies—cultural, economic, political, integrative—as the organizing principles for sub-systems. Around these exigencies systematic interaction among structures crystallizes. For certain purposes it is permissible to treat one or more social sub-systems as "closed"; we can inquire into the relations among economic units alone, for instance, without referring to the political sub-system of society. As we shall see, however, there is continuous interaction among sub-systems at their analytic boundaries. Sometimes we cannot ignore this interaction; we cannot understand the internal relations among economic units, for instance, without inquiring into political policies.

The economy may be treated as a social sub-system in that it constitutes the mutual interrelations among units involved in the production, distribution, and consumption of scarce goods and services. One important complex of units is found in the supply of the factors of production. At one boundary of the economy, structures such as higher education and science specialize in providing knowledge and technology, which are among the *land* factors. At another boundary, household units and educational institutions supply motivated and skilled individuals, or *labor*. At a third boundary, banks, governments, and private lenders specialize in the supply of *capital*. And finally, individual entrepreneurs, government agencies, and other structures generate a supply of *organizational principles* to the economy. These factors of production feed into the firm at a rate determined by supply-and-demand conditions, and combine to produce goods and services. Thereafter the firm interacts with consumers—also via supply-and-demand mechanisms—and disposes of products for price payments.

An economic system may be represented in different ways. In the last paragraph we spoke of relations among structural units. For purposes of analysis, we might wish to distill out certain quantifiable by-products generated in the interaction among these structures. For example, Keynes chose as his effective behaving units the variables of consumption, investment, and savings. His choice of variables does not conflict with the representation of the economy as a systematic set of relations among structural units; it is merely a representation of processes at a different level of abstraction.

The political system is a second example of a social sub-system. The key structure in the political system is a collectivity responsible for generating binding political decisions. This structure is involved in interactive relations with two other structural complexes. First, the decision-making unit interacts with the suppliers of factors that make for political effectiveness—with economic units that supply (mainly through taxation) facilities for implementing decisions through administration; with the electorate, interest groups, lobbies, and the like, that supply support for the political unit; and with the public at large which supplies legitimacy for the political system. Second, the decision-making political unit interacts with those who make diverse demands on it to produce policies and implement these policies. In the polity, as well as the economy, then, it is possible to represent the various structural units—public, decision-making units—as standing in systematic relations with one another.

The concept of system can be applied at many levels other than the societal level, from which the two preceding examples are drawn. Indeed, it is possible to view the economy as the parent system, and analyze its constituent clusters of activities—production, investment, innovation, and so on—as themselves constituting sub-systems. Then, within the economy, we could take a more concrete structure, such as a market or a firm, and analyze it in terms of some of the basic functional exigencies of social systems. The concrete units of structure differ at each level of system-reference, but the principles of system analysis are identical.

In our subsequent analysis, the concept of sanctions will come to occupy an extremely important place. In Chapter 2 we defined sanctions as referring to the use of social resources—in their significance both as rewards and deprivations—to control the behavior of persons in social structures. Classifications of sanctions parallel classifications of social structures and social systems. Correspondingly, the following types of sanctions are available for social control:

1. *Economic rewards and deprivations.* This refers to the system of wages, salaries, and profits that can be employed in determining the role distribution in a society, the recruitment of individuals into these roles, and the degree of effort elicited within these roles.

2. *Political measures.* These include physical coercion, the threat of coercion, influence, bargaining, the promise of political power, and so on.

3. *Integrative measures.* One focus of integrative pressure is particularism, or membership in some ascriptive group. Membership in a kinship grouping, for instance, not only may set up expectations with respect to roles that a given member may assume, but also may determine the conditions of entry and tenure in a role. Group membership may also be important for controlling a person once he has assumed a role. The key feature of particularistic sanctions of this sort is that the sanctioner appeals to the integrative ties (membership) of the actor in question. Other foci of particularism besides kinship are caste membership, tribal affiliation, membership in ethnic groups, and so on.

4. *Value commitments.* In this case commitment to fundamental principles is the lever that is used to induce individuals to enter roles and behave in certain ways once in them. Specific areas in which fundamental values operate as sanctions are in religious doctrine, nationalism, anticolonialism, socialism, and communism, or any combination of these.

Such are the sanctions that parallel the major varieties of social sub-systems. From one angle, sanctions are distinctive *products* of one particular type of social sub-system. The economic system, for instance, produces

38

wealth, which can be used as a sanction in many social contexts; the political system produces power, another generalized sanction; the religious-kinship complex produces value commitments. From another angle, sanctions produced in one sub-system constitute *resources* for other social sub-systems. Wealth, for instance, is one of the basic resources acquired and utilized by political and religious structures to agument their effectiveness. The various social sub-systems of a society are thus linked by a series of complex interchanges of resources, or sanctions.

In this chapter we shall investigate the relations between the economy and the other three sub-systems of society we have identified: (1) The cultural sub-system. In particular, what is the economic significance of values and ideologies? (2) The political sub-system. How is the economy related politically to many parts of its environment—to laborers, stockholders, the government, and so on? (3) The integrative sub-system. In particular, what is the economic significance of two types of solidary groupings—kinship and ethnic?

In addition, we shall analyze briefly a few relations between the economy and *stratification*. This social phenomenon lies on a different analytic level from the social sub-systems outlined. By stratification we mean simply that for any social structure some roles receive more rewards than others. Thus it is possible to describe the distribution of all relevant sanctions in a social system. The results of such a description are statements of the distribution of wealth, the distribution of power, the distribution of religious rewards (e.g., grace), and so on. Sometimes it is possible to speak of the stratification of individuals (i.e., by calculating their differential receipts of rewards), of organizations, or of whole classes (peasants, proletarians). In any case, whatever our basis for describing the differential distribution of sanctions in society, stratification is intimately related to the economic life of the society—to the motivation of economic agents, to the ways individuals spend their income, and so on. So we shall treat stratification as an important aspect of the non-economic world.

The Concrete Structuring of Economic Activities

As to the type of behavior they control, sanctions are non-specific. It is possible, for instance, to move people to perform economic actions by using non-economic sanctions. Consider the following: (1) Suppose I am in the process of moving from one house to another. One of the economic tasks that faces me is to transfer heavy furniture and kitchen appliances. Rather than hire the moving van to transfer them, I decide to ask my brother for help. In this case I am using common membership bonds as a sanction to induce another person to perform an economic task. (2) Suppose I am passing through customs and am caught with too many bottles of wine. The customs official threatens to confiscate the illegal amount. I bribe the official and get my way. In this way I am using economic sanctions to induce another person to engage in (or in this case, to refrain from engaging in) a political action.

Add to these simple examples a more complicated one from our own economy. Broadly speaking, the following sanctions are operative in establishing interactive relations between business and labor: (1) fundamental values, such as free enterprise and success, which are inculcated in potential incumbents of occupational roles during periods of early socialization

the economy and other social sub-systems

and education; (2) monetary compensation, by which individuals are induced to enter particular jobs in the market; (3) political contests between interest groups, particularly labor and management, by which general wage levels are regulated; (4) use of more centralized political and legal machinery for regulating occupational life, usually when the second and third principles seem to be functioning inadequately. In general, these sanctions are not highly centralized in our society; a single agency is *not* presumed to have direct control over the education of children, the operation of the labor market, the settlement of industrial disputes.

One key question in considering the structure of economic life, then, is the degree to which specifically economic sanctions such as price—as against other sanctions (political, membership criteria)—operate as direct controls over economic activity. In America economic sanctions are important and are conspicuously institutionalized in an extensive market structure. In the Soviet Union economic sanctions have a significant place, but in most spheres the use of money and the establishment of prices are subordinated to centralized political controls. In many primitive societies economic sanctions such as money are scarcely developed, and much of economic life is conducted as an aspect of kinship obligations and religious ritual.

A second key question concerning the structure of economic activities involves the locus of control over the sanctions themselves. This question overlaps with the problem of political sanctions as such, but rests at a higher level of generality. Consider, for example, several different types of economic activity. In an ideal-type paternalistic industrial setting, the industrial manager has at his disposal both economic and political (and perhaps even moral) sanctions to recruit and control employees. In an ideal-type free-enterprise system, the industrial manager has only economic sanctions to recruit employees, but once they are recruited, he has limited political authority over them. In an ideal-type totalitarian system, the industrial manager may utilize both economic and political sanctions, but for both he is held accountable to a centralized political source.

In these introductory sections we have developed a number of concepts—system, structure, sanctions, and so on—which provide an apparatus with which we may now deal with comparative variation in the structuring of economic activity and in the relations among economic and non-economic sub-systems.

The Economy and Cultural Factors

In considering cultural elements that affect and are affected by economic activity, we shall rely on the common distinction between the *evaluational* and the *existential* aspects of culture. By evaluational we refer to that which is considered desirable in a system of cultural values; that which ought to be pursued by members of a society. By existential we refer to assertions concerning what man, society, and nature are like. Thus, in a racist belief-system, the evaluational aspect is the affirmation that one race ought to reap a great advantage with respect to the good things of life; the existential (or we might say ideological) aspect is the assertion that the disinherited race is deserving of its lot because it is biologically inferior.

With regard to cultural beliefs about economic activities, then, we may ask two types of question: (1) Evaluational. Do economic activities

the economy and other social sub-systems

occupy a major place in the cultural value system? Whether major or minor, are they positively or negatively valued? Are they valued as an end in themselves, or viewed as subordinated to the pursuit of national power, the attainment of a state of religious bliss, or the consolidation of a lineage? (2) Existential. What is the nature of man? Is he defined as being economically motivated, or are these features of his existence underplayed? What is the nature of society? Does it provide opportunities for economic activity, or is this defined as being impossible in the good society? After having established answers to these questions for any set of cultural beliefs —with due allowance for regional and class variations—we are better able to analyze the relations between values and ideologies on the one hand and economic activities on the other.

What is the character of these relations? Unfortunately it is impossible to formulate definite principles; we must be content with specifying those few relations that have been isolated through careful empirical research. Accordingly, the following four significant associations between economic and cultural life have been stressed:

Values as Independent Variables
that Facilitate or Inhibit Economic Activity

Max Weber, the outstanding analyst of the independent significance of religion in the encouragement of rational economic activity, argued that the themes of this-worldly asceticism developed so highly in Protestantism and especially Calvinism encouraged man to value highly the rational and methodical mastery of the social and cultural, and in particular the economic environment. The great Oriental religions— especially the classical Chinese and the classical Indian—did not, on the other hand, offer such an encouraging cultural framework for the rational pursuit of economic gain.[1] While Weber clearly did not argue for a one-sided causal view of the relations between religion and economic activity, his analysis contrasts with that of Karl Marx, who treated religious beliefs as elements of the superstructure and thus generally dependent on the operative forces in a society's economic structure.

The "Weber thesis" has stimulated much analysis of the economic implications of religious systems other than those that Weber himself studied.[2] Other analysts have argued that secular beliefs, especially nationalism, exert an even more direct force on economic development. As Kingsley Davis argues:

> . . . nationalism is a *sina qua non* of industrialization, because it provides people with an overriding, easily acquired, secular motivation for making painful changes. National strength or prestige becomes the supreme goal, industrialization the chief means. The costs, inconveniences, sacrifices, and loss of traditional values can be justified in terms of this transcending, collective ambition. The new collective entity, the nation-state, that sponsors and grows from this aspiration is equal to the exi-

[1] Relevant works include *The Protestant Ethic and the Spirit of Capitalism* (London: Allen & Unwin, 1948); *The Religion of China* (Glencoe, Ill.: The Free Press, 1951); *The Religion of India* (Glencoe, Ill.: The Free Press, 1958).

[2] An outstanding example is found in Robert N. Bellah, *Tokugawa Religion* (Glencoe, Ill.: The Free Press, 1957); a recent minor study is found in Robert E. Kennedy, Jr., "The Protestant Ethic and the Parsis," *American Journal of Sociology* (1962), 68: 11–20.

gencies of industrial complexity; it draws directly the allegiance of every citizen, organizing the population as one community; it controls the passage of persons, goods, and news across the borders; it regulates economic and social life in detail. To the degree that the obstacles to industrialization are strong, nationalism must be intense to overcome them.[3]

In fact, nationalism seems in many cases to be the very instrument designed to smash those traditional religious systems which Weber himself found less permissive than Protestantism for economic activity.

On the other hand, nationalism, like many traditionalistic religious systems, may hinder economic advancement by "reaffirmation of traditionally honored ways of acting and thinking," by fostering anti-colonial attitudes after they are no longer relevant, and, more indirectly, by encouraging passive expectations of "ready-made prosperity." [4] In short, some types of values encourage economic development; others discourage it; and still others seem to have different significances at different levels of development. We do not yet know the kinds of situation in which each effect will be apparent. We shall, however, return to the problem when we discuss secularization in Chapter 5.

Ideology as Moral Justification of Existing Arrangements

One of the distinguishing features of the human being is that he is a user of symbols, and that he uses these symbols to assign meaning to the social relations into which he enters. The term "ideology" often refers to those assertions about the nature of the persons in a social situation and their relations to one another. The functions of ideologies are many. They give a broader meaning to activities that otherwise might not be immediately intelligible; or, more strongly, they may be used to induce people in a system of social relations that they should do things they might not otherwise wish to do.

Perhaps the most thorough study of the "control" aspects of ideology is Reinhard Bendix' comparative study of managerial ideologies as they have developed in four industrializing countries—Great Britain, the United States, Russia, and East Germany.[5] Bendix' main concern is with the justifications that managerial classes have generated in the process of inducing workers to submit to their authority. Moreover, he attempts to account for these ideologies in terms of the current requirements of the industrial framework; thus he traces the development of the "human relations" ideology to the double function of proclaiming the legitimate rights of management as well as assisting managers to achieve coordination within their enterprises. Clearly the dominant function of ideology in Bendix' view is to legitimize and defend growing or existing institutional arrangements.

[3] "Social and Demographic Aspects of Economic Development in India," in Simon Kuznets, Wilbert E. Moore, and Joseph J. Spengler (eds.), *Economic Growth: Brazil, India, Japan* (Durham: Duke University Press, 1955), p. 294.

[4] Bert F. Hoselitz, "Non-economic Barriers to Economic Development," *Economic Development and Cultural Change* (1952–1953), 1: 9; Hoselitz, "Nationalism, Economic Development, and Democracy," *Annals of the Academy of Political and Social Science* (May 1956), 305: 1–11.

[5] *Work and Authority in Industry* (New York: Wiley, 1596); for a brief summary statement, see Bendix, "Industrialization, Ideologies, and Social Structure," *American Sociological Review* (1959), 24: 613–632.

the economy and other social sub-systems

Ideology as Moral Attack
on Existing Arrangements

In industrial disputes management typically defends its position with ideological assertions concerning the principles of free enterprise in the collective-bargaining relationship and with parallel assertions of management's interest in the welfare of the worker. On the side of the union, a counter-ideology develops, which also "represent self-justifications of union objectives":

> The [self-justification] of the largest scope is the contention that trade-unions are instruments of social justice. The second moral justification underlying American unionism is that it protects the individual worker in his immediate work environment from exploitation and degradation.[6]

Thus in situations of conflict or social change, we frequently observe the development of two opposing ideologies, one used to defend and the other to attack and change existing arrangements. Interestingly, two such opposing ideologies have developed in the field of industrial sociology itself. The older ideology, labeled by Robert Stone as the "Conflict of Interest" approach, is emphasized more by economists, political scientists, and historians. Adherents to this approach to industrial relations stress that conflict based on economic motives is a normal state of affairs in the economic system; furthermore, they assume that this conflict should lead to changes in the institutional order. The second ideology, called the "Human Relations" approach, has been developed by sociologists mainly in the past three decades. Adherents to this ideology emphasize cooperation at the factory level as the normal state of affairs, stress good communication, and generally accept existing institutional arrangements.[7] While the contrast is perhaps too simple, it is true that these two loosely defined schools have lived for a long time in bitter opposition to one another.

Ideology as a Device
to Ease Situations of Strain

Many commentators have indicated that ideologies tend to flourish in situations in which there is a discrepancy between a set of ideal standards and an actual state of affairs.[8] Several studies of the American business ideology lend some support to this view. Francis X. Sutton, *et al.*, in a study of the American business creed, attributed the tenacity of the free-enterprise myth among businessmen to various strains in their roles; for example, their own ambivalence toward the phenomenon of bigness in the American economy is smoothed over by a defiant reassertion of the values of traditional free enterprise.[9] Sigmund Diamond, in a study of the treatment of American entrepreneurs in the press during the past 150 years, argues that the pervasive tendency to deify leading business-

[6] Arthur Kornhauser, Robert Dubin, and Arthur M. Ross, "Problems and Viewpoints," in *Industrial Conflict* (New York: McGraw-Hill, 1954), pp. 18–19.
[7] Robert C. Stone, "Conflicting Approaches to the Study of Worker-Manager Relations," *Social Forces* (1952–1953), 31: 117–124.
[8] Talcott Parsons, *The Social System* (Glencoe, Ill.: The Free Press, 1951), pp. 289–297.
[9] *The American Business Creed* (Cambridge: Harvard University Press, 1956), pp. 58–64.

men was in part an effort to counter the public ambivalence toward business leaders.[10] Ely Chinoy, in a study of automobile workers, asserts that "industrial workers . . . are caught between the promises of a widely affirmed tradition [the Horatio Alger myth] and the realities of the contemporary economic and social order [i.e., blocked social mobility]." One common reaction to this situation of strain, Chinoy argues, is for workers to "reconcile their limited aspirations with the cultural imperative to aim high and persevere by redefining 'getting ahead,' by focusing their ambitions on their children, and by verbally retaining the illusion of small business ambitions." [11]

Such are some of the functions of ideology in economic life—to justify existing economic arrangements, to attack them, and to ease strains in them. Future research should focus on the social conditions under which each of these functions of ideology is most pronounced. Perhaps the most promising line of research is to inquire into the different functions of ideology during different phases of social change. Early in the development of any given ideology—e.g., *laissez faire*—its major function is likely to be to attack traditional economic arrangements. Then, as the ideology becomes relatively established, its dominant functions turn to the defense of existing arrangements and to the smoothing over of strains that arise in roles institutionalized in the name of ideology itself.

The Economy and Political Variables

In this volume we shall examine the political involvements of economic units through a series of expanding circles: (1) Political relations within the productive unit, including the institutionalization of authority and the emergence of conflict. We shall take this up in Chapter 4. (2) Political relations among productive units, which raises the subject of imperfect competition and the concentration of wealth. (3) Political relations between productive units as an aggregate and the immediate economic environment. We shall mention firms' relations with consumers and stockholders, and devote considerable attention to labor-management relations, a favorite subject in economic sociology. (4) Political relations between productive units as an aggregate and government.

Political Relations among Firms

Most of the written material on the concentration of economic power centers on three themes. The first is formal economic analysis of the patterns of imperfect competition, and the implications of these patterns for price, output, wasted resources, and the like. The second is policy-oriented discussions on unfair competition, price-cutting, price-leadership, and methods of regulating these phenomena. The third is discussions of the degree of concentration of wealth and power in the economy, and the social and political implications of this concentration. With reference to the American economy, for instance, Carl Kaysen has summarized the situation as follows:

[10] *The Reputation of the American Businessman* (Cambridge: Harvard University Press, 1955), pp. 178–179.
[11] Ely Chinoy, *Automobile Workers and the American Dream* (Garden City, N. Y.: Doubleday, 1955), p. 4; and "The Tradition of Opportunity and the Aspirations of Automobile Workers," *American Journal of Sociology* (1951–1952), 57: 453.

the economy and other social sub-systems

[Figures of employment, allocation of defense contracts, assets, etc.] show clearly that a few large corporations are of overwhelmingly disproportionate importance in our economy, and especially in certain key sectors of it. Whatever aspect of their economic activity we measure . . . we see the same situation. Moreover, it is one which has been stable over a period of time. The best evidence . . . is that the degree of concentration has varied little for the three or four decades before 1947. . . .[12]

Some of the well-known consequences of the increasing size of firms and increasing concentration of wealth and power are the tendency to squeeze smaller, less efficient enterprises out of the market (the small retail grocery store, which has suffered greatly at the hands of the supermarket, is perhaps the most recent victim); the relatively great ability of the large firm to accumulate large capital reserves and to finance "lumpy" investments and large-scale research; and the tendency for competition among very large firms to manifest itself in advertising, not pricing.

Less is known about the operative determinants of a firm's investment, production, and pricing behavior as it increases in size and control of the market. We might suggest, however, that the active determinants in the behavior of small firms with less or no control over the market are the state of demand for their products and the availability of capital for them to invest. As the size of the firm increases, its immediate capital problem recedes more into the background; if the firm controls a portion of the market, even demand ceases to be as active as a determinant in their behavior. At such a point their production and pricing policy comes to be more oriented to the behavior of other firms in the industry. Thus economic behavior comes to reflect more and more the political relations among firms. When the firm comes to be a super-firm (as in the case of General Motors or General Electric), the most active determinant in its environment is neither the state of the market nor the behavior of other firms but the attitude of the government, which may be interested in trust-busting, regulating behavior, passing new tax laws, and so on.

Political Relations with the Immediate Economic Environment: Consumers. The political relations between business enterprise and consumers are manifested chiefly in market relations. Under conditions of perfect competition neither the firm nor the consumer has power to control price and output in the market. With the advent of the concentration of economic power in the productive sector, however, this situation gives way to an asymmetry which favors the producing unit. Whatever organized resistance to this asymmetrical situation the consumers have been able to muster in the modern complex economy has taken the following two forms:

1. Political agitation as consumers for regulation of prices and standards and control of unfair competition. This is not direct action on the part of the consumers, but action through the formal governmental structure.

2. The establishment of consumers' cooperatives to distribute goods and services. Although the consumers' cooperative movement has mani-

---

[12] "The Corporation: How Much Power? What Scope?" in Edward S. Mason (ed.), *The Corporation in Modern Society* (Cambridge: Harvard University Press, 1959), p. 88. For an analysis of the similarity of pattern of concentration between the United States and Great Britain, cf. P. Sargent Florence, *The Logic of British and American Industry* (London: Routledge and Kegan Paul, 1953), pp. 22–36.

fested itself in almost every country, it has rarely been a significant economic force.

Stockholders. In terms of the relations between productive firm and stockholders, managers in recent times have consolidated political power at the level of the firm. In 1932 A. A. Berle, Jr., and Gardiner Means (*The Modern Corporation and Private Property*) sketched the main lines of this consolidation. Their main thesis was that ownership of corporate property and control of the firm's economic decisions had been increasingly separated. Before the mid-nineteenth century the political control of the business enterprise lay in the hands of the individual or small group who owned all the property used as capital in the enterprise. With the rise of the corporate form, however, ownership was dispersed among stockholders only remotely connected with the day-to-day management of the enterprise. Control of the decisions within the corporation had come to rest more and more in the hands of professional managers, whose actual ownership rights were minimal. Since the Berle and Means analysis, the power of the managers has apparently become even more marked. Eugene V. Rostow recently summarized the current situation:

> The current prototype, increasingly, is that of a corporation with stock widely scattered among individuals, investment trusts, or institutional investors, who faithfully vote for the incumbent management, and resolutely refuse to participate in its concerns. In such companies, the stockholders obey the management, not the management the stockholders. Most stockholders of this class are interested in their stock only as investments. The prevalence of this view makes it almost hopeless to expect that the electoral process can ever become anything more significant than an empty ritual.[13]

Labor. We now turn to a more extended treatment of those political involvements of productive enterprises that have received the most study in economic sociology—relations with labor. This great interest is traceable in part to continual conflict in labor-management relations and in part to the sympathy that many social scientists (who are usually liberal) sustain with the aims of organized labor.

We shall begin by outlining a number of structural variations in labor-management relations. The most advantageous way of detailing these variations is to ask: In what other structures are the economic relations between labor and its employers embedded?

One of the typical forms of labor organization before the industrial revolution in England (about the mid-eighteenth century) was the "friendly society." These clubs of workmen were interested in exercising political influence over masters with regard to apprenticeship, wages, and the quality of goods produced; but they served a number of other social functions as well. They were repositories for workers' savings; they were insurance societies against death, illness, and the like; they were convivial drinking clubs. And above all they displayed a tendency to unite with the masters frequently with regard to the welfare of the industry as a whole. The friendly society, then, was a kind of multi-functional organization, standing in relative solidarity with the masters.

---

[13] Eugene V. Rostow, "To Whom and for What Ends is Corporate Management Responsible?" in Mason (ed.), *op. cit.*, pp. 53–54.

the economy and other social sub-systems

With the increasing separation of the worker from his capital and his product during the years of the Industrial Revolution, the character of trade unionism also began to change. During the first half of the nineteenth century in Britain, more specialized unions—unions particularly interested in wages and definitely opposed to the employing class—began to emerge. These became the typical form of union in both Great Britain and the United States in the nineteenth century.

In a variety of ways labor-management relations are fused with the larger political structures of society. The extreme case of fusion is found in totalitarian countries—such as Nazi Germany or the Soviet Union—in which open and free collective bargaining over wage matters is ruled out, and even grievance procedure is carried out under a centralized political rubric. In some instances the labor unions operate in part as an arm of government and management interests; they may assist in educating and disciplining workers.[14] A less extreme (but sometimes similar) pattern is found in many underdeveloped countries. While the governments of these countries are sympathetic to organized labor and enlist its political support in principle, strong governmental controls over organized labor are frequently and severely exercised in practice. "Compulsory arbitration is widespread, strikes are sometimes forcibly broken, and union demands are denounced by government leaders." [15] Still another variant of fusion with political structures is found in countries with a portion of their major industries nationalized (such as modern Great Britain). While the trade unions in such countries maintain their autonomy, they now deal with governmental officials as managers. The whole situation in nationalized industries is complicated, moreover, by the fact that the impetus to nationalization frequently came from political parties which represented, or had the full backing of, organized labor.[16]

Labor-management relations are sometimes profoundly influenced by a fusion with particular ethnic groupings. The bitter antagonism and the extraordinary degree of violence in the Pennsylvania mine disorders—known as the Molly Maguire Riots—in the 1870's can be traced in part to the Irish origins of the miners.[17] The peculiar character of labor-management relations in the California agricultural system of contract labor can also be traced in part to the domination of the labor force during different periods by the Chinese, the Japanese, and the Mexicans—each with distinctive traditions of social organization and attitudes toward authority.[18]

Finally, labor organizations are frequently fused with collective move-

[14] For a sample account of labor-management relations in such countries, cf. Matthew A. Kelley, "Industrial Relations in National Socialist Germany," and Walter Galenson, "Soviet Russia," in Kornhauser, Dubin, and Ross (eds.), *op. cit.,* pp. 467–477 and 478–486; Emily Clark Brown, "Labor Relations in Soviet Factories," *Industrial and Labor Relations Review* (1957–1958), 11: 183–202.

[15] Felicia J. Deyrup, "Organized Labor and Government in Underdeveloped Countries: Sources of Conflict," *Industrial and Labor Relations Review* (1958–1959), 12: 104.

[16] For an account of the collective bargaining machinery in the British coal industry after nationalization, cf. George B. Baldwin, *Beyond Nationalization: The Labor Problems of British Coal* (Cambridge: Harvard University Press, 1955), pp. 63–69.

[17] J. Walter Coleman, *The Molly Maguire Riots* (Richmond, Va.: Garrett and Massie, 1936), pp. 19–39.

[18] Lloyd H. Fisher, *The Harvest Labor Market in California* (Cambridge: Harvard University Press, 1953), especially pp. 24–37.

the economy and other social sub-systems

ments, such as anarchism, syndicalism, socialism, home-rule, anti-colonialism, and nationalism. This fusion has always characterized continental Europe to a much greater degree than the Anglo-Saxon world, and in contemporary times many of the nationalist movements of the underdeveloped areas are thoroughly entangled with the labor movements of these countries.[19]

Closely related to the different structuring of labor-management relations are the different forms that conflict between labor and management can take. In a fairly exhaustive classification, Kornhauser, Ross, and Dubin list the following types:

I. Manifestations of organized group conflict (union-management conflicts).
   A. In industry.
      1. Interruptions of production—strikes, lockouts, and removal of plant.
      2. Organized restrictions of output—work limitations, slow-downs, sabotage, and unilateral changes of work standards, piece rates, etc.
      3. Conflicts in contract negotiations, grievance cases, dealings between foremen and stewards, etc., without work stoppages.
   B. In the larger society.
      1. Political opposition—local and national.
      2. Other community and social oppositions—conflicting pressures on newspapers and radio, rivalries over recreational, educational, and other services for workers.
II. Manifestations of individual and unorganized conflict.
   A. In industry—employee behavior.
      1. Unorganized withholding of effort, intentional waste and inefficiency, etc.
      2. Labor turnover and absenteeism.
      3. Complaints, friction, infractions of rules, and similar evidences of low morale and discontent.
   B. In industry—management behavior.
      1. Autocratic supervision and overstrict discipline and penalties.
      2. Unnecessary and discriminatory firing, layoffs, and demotions.
      3. Unofficial speed-ups, etc.
   C. In the larger society.
      1. Employee expressions of opposition in everyday talk, voting behavior, consumer choices, etc.
      2. Owner and management expressions of opposition in use of political influence against unions, support of one-sided educational and propaganda programs, etc.[20]

A central issue in the study of labor-management relations is this: When does one rather than another form of industrial conflict appear? Although very little research has been done on this subject, it is apparent that the *structure* of labor-management relations is crucial in determining the

---

[19] George T. Daniel, "Labor and Nationalism in the British Caribbean," *Annals of the American Academy of Political and Social Science* (March 1957), 310: 162–171; J. Henry Richardson, "Indonesian Labor Relations in their Political Setting," *Industrial and Labor Relations Review* (1958–1959), 12: 56–78.

[20] "Problems and Viewpoints," in Kornhauser, Dubin, and Ross (eds.), *op. cit.*, pp. 14–15.

type of industrial conflict. Consider the following illustrations of this principle:

1. In settings where central political control sharply limits the range of conflict and where the political authorities appear to be capricious, informal channels for handling grievances often develop. In a study of Soviet grievance procedures, Janusz Zawodny described such a situation:

> It seems clear that the workers hesitated to claim their admissible grievances. This was because formal agencies within a plant and the members of these bodies were repeatedly able to make an about-face on an issue whenever politically convenient and to attach an invidious political label to a worker's claim, the chosen manner of settlement, and the outcome. The members of the formal agencies could circumvent the law themselves in order to secure a satisfactory solution for the workers, particularly when such settlement could be used as an incentive. Conversely, the same type of grievance could receive the reverse treatment when a display of "socialistic vigilance" was deemed necessary for "educational purposes." [21]

Such an atmosphere of uncertainty discourages an open and literal presentation of grievances. What settlements do occur seem not to rest immediately on formal machinery but rather on particularistic loyalties (friends, contacts); "workers used formal agencies as an official screen for the exchange of mutual assistance and the application of influence—these under the aegis of unwritten mutual amnesty." [22]

2. Insofar as a labor movement is an adjunct of a political party, this encourages the appearance of conflicts "in the larger society," especially electoral conflict, attempts to enact legislation favorable to one of the parties in conflict, and so on.

3. Insofar as a labor movement is an adjunct of a revolutionary political movement, the use of the strike will be less for economic gain (as it is in business unionism), and more for political attack against the constituted authorities. In the ideology of communism and syndicalism, for instance, the strike is avowedly a political weapon.

4. Limited evidence indicates that in some cases the appearance of one form of conflict leads to a decline in other forms. K.G.J.C. Knowles reports on research on the British coal-mining industry, which suggests that "irrespective of the differences between years and the differences between districts, if strike losses are high absenteeism losses tend to be low and vice versa." Two factors probably account for this effect: First, insofar as strikes cost laborers both wages and savings, they cannot afford to be absent from work during periods of collective strife; second, insofar as involvement in strikes generally heightens worker solidarity, workers may come to the work place more frequently in order to be with other workers. The negative relation between different forms of conflict is, however, probably limited to certain types of situations; Knowles suggests that if labor unrest is very acute, both strikes and absenteeism may be high.[23]

---

[21] "Grievance Procedures in Soviet Factories," *Industrial and Labor Relations Review* (1956–1957), 10: 553.

[22] *Ibid.* For the development of a network of informal contacts in the Soviet productive sphere as well, see below, pp. 83–84.

[23] *Strikes* (Oxford: Basil Blackwell, 1952), p. 225.

5. The forms of labor conflict have displayed broad changes in the history of Anglo-American unionism, and these changes are associated with structural changes in unionism itself. It is possible to identify three broad phases. First, in the earliest stages of development of the labor force, conflict tends to take two forms—individual protest, in the form of high turnover, absenteeism, sabotage, irregular hours, and so on; and spontaneous collective protests, such as mob violence, destruction of machinery by raids, and quickly-organized, chaotic strikes. The conflict rests in part on the severe strains that industrialization brings to the working populace; its particular form of manifestation, however, rests on the fact that in the absence of worker organization conflict is not institutionalized and therefore appears in the form of individual expression or spontaneous group outbursts.[24]

Second, in the "middle period" of labor development, conflict alternated between the use of strikes for economic gain and more dispersed forms of conflict. This alternation, moreover, followed the business cycle. During the nineteenth century, for instance, labor agitation in the United States followed a rough cyclical pattern; "it . . . centered on economic or trade union prosperity only to change abruptly to 'panaceas' and politics with the descent of depression." [25] During prosperity, when labor was scarce, workers could use demands for wage increases and strikes effectively; furthermore, they could finance union organizations and periods of idleness more readily. During depressions these methods became less effective, and workers turned to demands for protective legislation from the government or to grandiose schemes such as cooperation to build a new economic structure.

Third, in very recent times, "business unionism" has emerged. Unions have tended to rationalize the conduct of the strike, reduce violence, discipline the workers, localize strikes, minimize secondary strikes, reduce unnecessary damage to industry, and protect unions in the face of public opinion. Much of the heat and emotion has disappeared from strikes, and whatever revolutionary overtones strikes might once have had, they have clearly diminished in mid-twentieth century. Peaceful collective bargaining has become the standard form of conflict. Spontaneity and violence appear to be limited to the "unofficial strike" or "wildcat strike," in which groups of workers not only feel grievances toward management but also feel they are isolated or receiving the "run-around" from big unions or big government.[26]

Because the structure of labor-management relations partly determines the form of industrial conflict, it becomes difficult to compare the rates of similar forms of conflict (e.g., the strike) in different structural contexts. Nevertheless, some revealing studies of the differential incidence of

[24] Clark Kerr, John T. Dunlop, Frederick H. Harbison, and Charles A. Myers, *Industrialism and Industrial Man* (Cambridge: Harvard University Press, 1960), pp. 209–210.

[25] Selig Perlman, *A History of Trade Unionism in the United States* (New York: Macmillan, 1937), pp. 141–142. Perhaps the two most notable utopian movements were the Grand National and the Knights of Labor. With the more permanent organization of the A.F.L. beginning in the 1880's and 1890's, greater continuity came to the activity of organized labor.

[26] Arthur M. Ross, "The Natural History of the Strike," in Kornhauser, Dubin, and Ross (eds.), *op. cit.*, pp. 30–36; Alvin W. Gouldner, *Wildcat Strike* (London: Routledge & Kegan Paul, 1955), p. 95; for an account of the development of unofficial strikes after nationalization in the British coal industry, cf. Baldwin, *op. cit.*, pp. 72–91.

50

strikes over time and among industries have appeared. One of the clearest findings is that by almost any measure—number of strikes, number of workers involved, or number of working-days lost—strikes seem to increase in prosperity and decline in depression.[27] We have already inquired into the structural reasons for this phenomenon. Strikes also appear to display seasonal variation within a single year. In his study of strikes in Great Britain between 1911 and 1947, Knowles found that strike rates peak in May and August (months of highest economic activity, especially in building, when conditions of "prosperity" hold). A slight decline was observable before holidays, a decline that presumably reflects the workers' increased need for cash during these times.[28]

Asking if certain industries are more strike-prone than others, Clark Kerr and Abraham Siegel conducted comparative research on strikes in eleven nations. They found a high propensity to strike in mining and maritime-longshore industries; medium high in lumber and textile industries; medium in chemical, printing, leather, general manufacturing, construction, and food industries; medium low in clothing, utilities, and services; and low in railroads, agriculture, and trade. Their first explanation of this differential distribution lay in the integration of the industrial workers among themselves and with the larger society. As the authors commented:

> (a) industries will be highly strike prone when the workers (i) form a relatively homogeneous group which (ii) is unusually isolated from the general community and which (iii) is capable of cohesion; and (b) industries will be comparatively strike free when their workers (i) are individually integrated into the larger society, (ii) are members of trade groups which are coerced by government or the market to avoid strikes, or (iii) are so individually isolated that strike action is impossible.[29]

Their second explanation, which fortifies the first, is that the isolated industries will tend to draw tough, combative workers because of the unpleasant, unskilled, and seasonal character of these industries.

The clustering of industrial disputes over time and among industries leads to the question of the causes of strikes. But we must first distinguish between the *issues* about which strikes are fought and the underlying *conditions* that give rise to them. The two are not always the same. Among the overt reason given in modern times for strike action and grievances, Charles Myers has distilled out the following four: (1) unfair or inadequate levels of wages; (2) unstable and irregular employment; (3) arbitrary and capricious management action—e.g., in discharging workers, in flouting union regulations; and (4) inadequate employee status and recognition.[30] Why one issue rather than another dominates a strike is a subject of interest, but the issue does not always reveal the cause. As Stanislas Wellisz puts it, "a number of strikes seemingly caused by wage disputes are really due to other factors, and wage demands are merely used as a rallying cry." [31] Among these "other factors," what are the most salient?

[27] Albert Rees, "Industrial Conflict and Business Fluctuations," *Journal of Political Economy* (1952), 60: 371–382; Knowles, *op. cit.*, pp. 145–150.

[28] Knowles, *op. cit.*, pp. 157–160.

[29] "The Interindustry Propensity to Strike—an International Comparison," in Kornhauser, Dubin, and Ross (eds.), *op. cit.*, p. 195.

[30] "Basic Employment Relations," in *ibid.*, p. 328.

[31] "Strikes in Coal-Mining," *British Journal of Sociology* (1953), 4: 355.

The fundamental causes of labor disputes can be divided into two classes: (1) permissive conditions, or the absence of obstacles to the ability to strike, and (2) sources of active unrest among the workers. Among the first the presence of labor organization is a strong encouragement to use the strike as a weapon; otherwise conflict is more likely to appear in individual or spontaneous group form. Furthermore, an organization in an isolated setting has even more striking power than one subjected to cross-pressures in a pluralistic community. In addition, the financial strength of workers' organizations is a major permissive factor; strikes occur with much greater frequency during periods of prosperity. Finally, strikes are more frequent when the government allows this type of expression, and less frequent when the government represses them, as in totalitarian states or in periods of national crisis.

As to the sources of active unrest among workers, we are confronted with a number of approaches that are the source of much controversy and confusion. Among the major competing explanations are the following:

1. The "economic advantage" school, which maintains that labor unions are "in business" and attempt to maximize the wage gains of their members.[32]

2. The "job security" school, which is a variant of the economic advantage school. It focuses on the desires of workmen to protect the conditions of their work in the long run rather than on short-term wage gains.[33]

3. The "class warfare" (or Marxist) school, which attributes worker unrest to the fact that the working classes suffer from systematic exploitation at the hands of the capitalists. This position has been stated in modified ways by various socialist historians of the labor movement.[34]

4. The "political" school, which emphasizes political conflict between unions and management over the recognition of unionism and collective bargaining, jurisdictional disputes among unions, internal leadership rivalries, and the influence of communism in unions.[35]

5. The "human relations" school, which is associated with the industrial sociology of Elton Mayo and his followers. Broadly speaking, this school traces basic dissatisfactions among laborers to the breakdown of primary groups among workers and the lack of communication and understanding between management and workers.[36]

Economic sociologists are currently at loggerheads over the relative merit of the basic causes of strikes. The strongest evidence for any one

[32] This position has been argued by John T. Dunlop in *Wage Determination under Trade Unions* (New York: Augustus M. Kelley, 1950).

[33] This school is associated with the name of Selig Perlman, who argued his case first in *A Theory of the Labor Movement* (New York: Macmillan, 1928).

[34] For a critique of the explanatory powers of this position with respect to the behavior of the British workers in the Industrial Revolution, cf. Neil J. Smelser, *Social Change in the Industrial Revolution* (Chicago: University of Chicago Press, 1959), pp. 389–399.

[35] Arthur M. Ross and Donald Irwin, "Strike Experience in Five Countries, 1927–1947: An Interpretation," *Industrial and Labor Relations Review* (1950–1951), 4: 323–342. Ross argues his case at greater length in *Trade Union Wage Policy* (Berkeley: University of California Press, 1948).

[36] John T. Dunlop and William Foote Whyte, "Framework for the Analysis of Industrial Relations: Two Views," *Industrial and Labor Relations Review* (1949–1950), 3: 383–401; Louis Schneider and Sverre Lysgaard, " 'Deficiency' and 'Conflict' in Industrial Sociology," *American Journal of Economics and Sociology* (1952–1953) 12: 49–61.

the economy and other social sub-systems

school is the plausible interpretation of one or several cases of industrial conflict. Surely the appropriate strategy at this time is to abandon the almost ideological positions that have crystallized around these schools, and investigate the specific conditions under which *each* kind of cause is most likely to be the active one in the genesis of strikes.

What are some of the ways of preventing industrial disputes from flaring into open conflict? In the relations between workers and managers themselves, management attempts to break strikes in the early stages of industrialization (through violence against unions, use of spies, use of paid agitators) have given way, especially since the late 1930's, to more moderate tactics—such as reliance on collective bargaining, and use of "better human relations programs, persuasion, and carefully chosen concessions." [37] Collective bargaining, in fact, has become the major vehicle for settling industrial disputes in modern times. On matters that arise during the time that elapses between major collective-bargaining agreements, grievance machinery has been very widely established; for matters of relatively minor concern, programs of "union-management cooperation" have made some headway.[38]

Several methods of preventing or minimizing the effects of industrial conflict involve the intervention of third parties. The most extreme form is direct government legislation or decree, which simply outlaws certain types of disputes; laws against strikes in the military and decrees against strikes in periods of national emergency are examples. The indiscriminate use of these extreme powers throughout a free economy, however, is not feasible. Nationalization, or intervention by assuming ownership of industry, does introduce a new principle of profit-sharing and thus possibly reduces some of the economic reasons for disputes; but those disputes arising out of work conditions, unemployment, and authority relations still occur.[39] More modest forms of third-party intervention are mediation and arbitration, both of which have been widely employed in the United States, but neither of which has proved to be without unanticipated problems in settling disputes.[40]

Finally, what have been the consequences of recent industrial conflicts? We may divide this question by considering the specific economic costs and consequences and the more general social consequences.

Since the middle 1920's a greater percentage of individual workers has been involved in strikes (largely because of the increasing size of unions); however, the shortening of strikes has diminished the loss of working time per worker. In ratio terms, the United States has suffered a greater proportion of lost working time through strikes than Sweden, Canada, Australia, or Great Britain. Even so, the total man-days of idleness through strikes in the United States between 1927 and 1955 (excluding work stop-

[37] Ross Stagner, *Psychology of Industrial Conflict* (New York: Wiley, 1956), p. 335.

[38] John T. Dunlop and James J. Healy, *Collective Bargaining*, rev. ed. (Homewood, Ill.: Irwin, 1955), pp. 53–64; Van D. Kennedy, "Grievance Negotiations," in Kornhauser, Dubin, and Ross (eds.), *op. cit.*, pp. 280–291; Robert Dubin, "Union-Management Co-operation and Productivity," *Industrial and Labor Relations Review* (1948–1949), 2: 195–209.

[39] T. E. Chester, "Industrial Conflicts in British Nationalized Industries," in Kornhauser, Dubin, and Ross (eds.), *op. cit.*, pp. 454–466.

[40] Edgar L. Warren, "Mediation and Fact Finding," and Irving Bernstein, "Arbitration," in Kornhauser, Dubin, and Ross (eds.), *op. cit.*, pp. 292–312.

pages in industries not directly involved) was considerably less than the man-days lost through unemployment in 1933 alone.[41] On the other hand, Neil Chamberlain and Jane Schilling have shown, by a careful analysis, that the impact of a strike on consumers and suppliers, among others, sometimes "constitutes the most important effects of a strike," more important certainly than the number of man-days lost.[42] Of course, to calculate when a strike costs the public more than it costs labor to forfeit the right to strike effectively poses enormous empirical and ethical problems.

The impact of union activity on wages can be discussed under two headings—general inflationary effects and labor's relative share of income. Apparently, unions augment inflationary tendencies. Their emphasis on full employment as a political issue has an indirect inflationary effect. In addition, if wages increase disproportionately to increases in workers' productivity—and if business compensates for this disproportion by raising prices—inflation results. Finally, insofar as unions are able to resist wage decreases, they augment the tendency toward high wage and price levels.[43]

How does union activity affect labor's share of national income? In cases where increased wages can be passed on to higher prices, the laborer's gain is negligible. In cases where full-employment policies lead to a rising cost of living, labor suffers, for it engages in a "chasing" relationship with rising prices. With regard to wage differentials between unionized and non-unionized workers, it is likely that union activity can raise the relative level of unionized workers' wages for a period, but over time the wage levels of others rise as fast (and in some cases faster, if demand conditions for unorganized labor are tight). In some industries labor can restrict labor supply and thus keep wages high. Finally, labor can agitate for governmental tax and welfare measures that redistribute income generally in favor of the lower-income groups; in England this political activity has accounted for almost all the redistributive effects in the past several decades.[44] From these counteractive effects of labor activity we conclude that in recent times the net effect of labor activity on its own share of income has been small.

With regard to the larger social consequences of industrial conflict, the *prima facie* conclusion is that the less the amount of conflict, the less the negative consequences for society. Some observers stress, however, that industrial conflict through controlled channels has stabilizing functions. As Clark Kerr argues,

> [Industrial conflict] assists in the solution of controversies, it may reduce intergroup tensions, and it may benefit the worker by balancing management power against union power. "Tactical" mediation can reduce aggressive industrial conflict, by decreasing industrial irrationality, by removing nonrationality, by aiding in the exploration of solutions, by abetting the parties in making graceful retreats, and by raising the cost of conflict, but its general contribution cannot be large; "strategical" mediation, or the

[41] Ross and Irwin, "Strike Experience in Five Countries," *op. cit.*, pp. 330–336; Kornhauser, Ross, and Dubin, "Problems and Viewpoints," *op. cit.*, pp. 7–8.

[42] *The Impact of Strikes* (New York: Harper, 1954), pp. 241–253.

[43] Lloyd G. Reynolds, *Labor Economics and Labor Relations*, 3rd ed. (Englewood Cliffs, N. J.: Prentice-Hall, 1960), pp. 314–316.

[44] For summary of research and discussion of this intricate issue, cf. Clark Kerr, "Trade-Unionism and Distributive Shares," *American Economic Review* (1954), 44: 279–292; Sumner H. Schlicter, "Do the Wage-Fixing Arrangements in the American Labor Market Have an Inflationary Bias?" *American Economic Review* (1954), 44: 322–346.

54

structuring of the environment, on the other hand, can effect major changes. It involves the better integration of workers and employers into society, the increased stability, the development of ideological compatibility, the arrangement of secure and responsive relationships among leaders and members, the dispersion of grievances, and the establishment of effective rules of the game.[45]

Political Relations
between Economic Units and Government

Among the major influences on the functioning of the economy are the relations between economic units and government. But a language for comparing different institutional arrangements with respect to these relations is poorly developed. The time-worn labels, "capitalist," "socialist," "communist," are unsatisfactory for many purposes. They overlook many midway cases (Is Great Britain capitalist or socialist?); they fail to catch colonial economies and highly traditionalist economies in their net (except by such stretched references as "primitive communism" or the "imperialist phase of capitalism"); worse yet, these terms are ideologically loaded.

One promising typology, however, stems from Bert Hoselitz' effort to compare and contrast the political dimensions of economic growth. Hoselitz mentions three fundamental polarities in describing the relations between government activity and economic activity:

1. Is the government engaged in *expansionist* activity—i.e., incorporating new territory and economic resources—or does it rely on the *intrinsic* productive resources of the existing political unit? The United States from 1830 to 1890 was clearly expansionist; Denmark is clearly intrinsic.

2. Is the political unit *dominant* over its own territory, or is it *satellitic* to some outside political unit? France and Germany in the nineteenth century were dominant; many colonized areas and Eastern European countries at present are satellitic.

3. Does the political unit allow economic activity to proceed in an *autonomous* way, or does it attempt to *induce* economic activity? Great Britain in the late eighteenth century is an autonomous case; the Soviet Union from the late 1920's to the present is an induced case.[46]

Hoselitz' concepts are more value-free than "capitalism," "socialism," and so on, and they include more types. Yet his scheme needs further refinement. Inducement, for instance, can take many forms; it can involve direct government ownership and day-by-day control (as in many communist countries); it can involve government ownership and only general policy control (as in the case of British nationalism); or it can rely on indirect influences, such as monetary and fiscal policy. Satellitic relations, again, may involve only economic dominance (as in the case of American influence on many Latin American countries), or it may involve territorial dominance as well (as did British, French, and Dutch colonialism in the late nineteenth and early twentieth centuries). In short, the comparative analysis of the relations between governments and economics is in need of refinement and elaboration of the dimensions to be used for such analysis.

[45] "Industrial Conflict and its Mediation," *American Journal of Sociology* (1954–1955), 60: 230–254.
[46] *Sociological Aspects of Economic Growth* (Glencoe, Ill.: The Free Press, 1960), pp. 85–114.

Much of the recent discussion of political-economic relations has focused on developments in the contemporary United States. As is well known, our society has a strong tradition of economic individualism and government non-intervention; hence governmental regulations in economic life are bound to be viewed with ambivalence. Thus, while many aspects of the contemporary situation are clear and well understood, much of the discussion is shrouded in confusion and controversy.

The classical *laissez-faire* period of the nineteenth century is over. The government, especially the federal government, has capitalized on the possibilities of constitutional intervention. Its activities include assistance, promotion, management, regulation, operation, and manipulation of economic activity. These activities extend into many corners—agriculture, old age, labor-management relations, workmen's compensation, commerce and business, natural resources, defense, and so on. Furthermore, the reasons for this growth of governmental power over the economy are fairly clear; it has been encouraged by the increasing need for coordination as the economy and social structure grow more complex, and by the increasingly thorny problem of securing justice and equality in the face of bigness. In addition, the past 50 years have been years of almost uninterrupted crisis—World War I, the Great Depression, World War II, and the Cold War—all calling for a high level of collective mobilization of resources.

Two features of these broad trends, however, are empirically unclear and are clouded by very strong feelings. The first feature concerns the implications of increasing governmental regulation for the traditional American values of individualism, equality of opportunity, and so on. Are we losing the frontier spirit? Does government welfare encourage passivity and lack of ambition? Are business and personal incentives destroyed by high levels of taxation? Such questions are the subject of heated and continuous debate. Yet so far as I know, not one systematic attempt even to refine these questions, much less to investigate them empirically, has been made.

The second feature concerns the degree of business influence *over* the government. One school of thought, advanced by the late C. Wright Mills, argues that political power has become increasingly concentrated in recent decades in the United States, and that the holders of power and makers of important decisions are a small group of corporate executives and military officials.[47] This view has been challenged on methodological grounds.[48] In addition, opposing interpretations have been offered. For instance, some social analysts have argued that while it may be true that the federal government has increased in absolute and even relative power, the sources of influence over the government have become more diversified than they were (say) in the late nineteenth century, when the business and financial communities appeared to occupy their strongest position of power relative to the government.[49] The resolution of this controversy is at best a complex

[47] See Mills' *The Power Elite* (New York: Oxford University Press, 1956), and *The Causes of World War III* (New York: Simon and Schuster, 1958).
[48] Robert A. Dahl, "A Critique of the Ruling Elite Model," *American Political Science Review* (1958), 52: 463–469.
[49] For different versions of this latter view, cf. John K. Galbraith, *American Capitalism: The System of Countervailing Power* (Boston: Houghton-Mifflin, 1952); David Riesman, Nathan Glazer, and Reuel Denney, *The Lonely Crowd* (Garden City, N.Y.: Doubleday, 1954), pp. 246–258; Talcott Parsons, "The Distribution of Power in American Society," in *Structure and Process in Modern Societies* (Glencoe, Ill.: The Free Press, 1960), pp. 199–225.

56

the economy and other social sub-systems

one. That neither corporate wealth nor private income has become notice-ably more concentrated (the latter has become less so) in the last five decades argues against Mills' position. The rise of big unionism and the maintenance of a strong agricultural bloc supports the pluralist rather than the elitist interpretation. On the other hand, the peculiar concentration of business and military power—occasioned by the enormous defense budget since the beginning of World War II—had a significant short-term impact on political decision-making.

Another issue in economic sociology concerns the character of business control over the political sphere at the local community level. Certainly in some types of community—such as the company town or the one-industry town—we would expect to have strong economic domination of political life. But in other types of communities—the sprawling metropolis, the suburban commuter town—we would expect to find a much more complex picture than domination by economic interest. In a boom town we would expect to find hardly any independent political sphere at all, except for an informal proliferation of vigilante justice.

The empirical research on economic controls over local politics shows a mixed picture. In a study of a southern community, Floyd Hunter found that the major decisions were guided by a small group of economically dominant individuals.[50] Delbert Miller, however, found conflicting evidence. Investigating the Hunter hypothesis that "business men (manufacturers, bankers, merchants, investment brokers, and large real estate holders) exert predominant influence in community decision-making," he compared the composition of "top influentials" in an American and English city, both similar in size to Hunter's metropolitan community. These influential citizens were dominated by business, but in the American city (located in the Pacific Northwest) and in the English city labor and educational elites were more significantly represented than in Hunter's city.[51] In a study of a Midwestern community, Robert Schulze found that over a 100-year period there emerged a tendency for a "withdrawal of the economic dominants from active and overt participation in . . . public life." Schulze attributed this change in part to the increasing control of economic affairs of the community from outside the community, leaving the running of local social and political affairs to "a group of middle-class business and professional people, none of whom are in economically dominant positions." [52]

Relations between the Economy and Solidary Groupings

Kinship refers to that complex of social relations that are calculated on the basis of the biological fact of birth and social fact of marriage. The family—and sometimes as the extended kinship unit (including grandparents, grandchildren, uncles, aunts, and cousins)—is the focus of some of the individual's most cohesive social ties. We shall consider kinship, then, as a first example of a solidary grouping.

[50] *Community Power Structure* (Chapel Hill: University of North Carolina Press, 1953).

[51] "Industry and Community Power Structure: A Comparative Study of an American and an English City," *American Sociological Review* (1958), 23: 9–15.

[52] "The Role of Economic Dominants in Community Power Structure," *American Sociological Review* (1958), 23: 3–9; also Ted C. Smith, "The Structuring of Power in a Suburban Community," *Pacific Sociological Review* (1960), 3: 83–88.

A second example of a solidary grouping is the ethnic group. In the United States, according to the Handlins' definition, "the ethnic group . . . is a loose agglomeration of individuals, aware of a common identity and organized in some degree in voluntary associations, which transmits a definable social and cultural heritage from generation to generation." The ethnic group is closely related to kinship, for "within [the ethnic group] the family plays an important role, for it is through the family that ethnic influences are extended in time."[53] In the United States, as elsewhere, the distinguishing characteristics of ethnic groups are color, national or regional origin, religion, or some combination of these.

Kinship Groupings

We find a rough structural congruence between type of family structure and type of economic activity. In an analysis of 549 cultures included in the "World Ethnographic Sample," Nimkoff and Middleton found the following associations:

> The independent family system tends to predominate in hunting and gathering societies, the extended family where there is a more ample and secure food supply. The extended family system tends to be associated with social stratification [of property], even when subsistence patterns are held constant. . . . The modern industrial society, with its small independent family, is . . . like the simpler hunting and gathering society and, in part, apparently for some of the same reasons, namely, limited need for family labor and physical mobility. The hunter is mobile because he pursues the game; the industrial worker, the job.[54]

One pervasive feature of tribal and peasant societies—whether the family system is independent or extended—is that economic roles tend to be subordinated to an individual's position in kinship roles. Specific economic duties are assigned to children up to a certain age, others accrue to him at adolescence, others at marriage; some are taken from him at the marriage of his son, and so on.[55] In modern society such age and sex regulation of economic activities persist in more limited forms (e.g., we exclude very young children from work and we expel old persons from economic roles through retirement).

These structural features of kinship and economic life are very general. How, more specifically, does kinship affect the course of economic life, and how is it affected by it? Or, otherwise, with reference to economic life, in what senses is kinship an independent variable, and in what senses a dependent variable?

Kinship structures encourage certain kinds of economic activity. The Japanese family system, for instance, through the rule of primogeniture, forced younger sons to leave the country for the city, where they

[53] Oscar Handlin and Mary F. Handlin, "Ethnic Factors in Social Mobility," *Explorations in Entrepreneurial History* (October 1956), 9: 1.

[54] M. F. Nimkoff and Russell Middleton, "Types of Family and Types of Economy," *American Journal of Sociology* (1960–1961), 66: 215–225.

[55] For two case studies of the intimate association between kinship roles and economic roles, cf. Meyer Fortes, *The Web of Kinship among the Tallensi* (New York: Oxford University Press, 1949); Conrad M. Arensberg and Solon T. Kimball, *Family and Community in Ireland* (Cambridge: Harvard University Press, 1940).

the economy and other social sub-systems

became possible candidates for factory labor.[56] A study of primogeniture in rural Ireland suggests that younger sons provided some candidates in the migration of young Irish males from the land.[57] In quite another economic context—commercial shipping—Bernard Bailyn has argued that:

> Kinship goes far in explaining the initiation of overseas trade in New England [during the seventeenth century] and the recruitment of the first New England merchants. Study of the family relations [especially intramarriage] in the second and third generations reveals the consolidation of these early mercantile families. And in the kinship ties secured between the established merchants and the post-Restoration commercial adventurers one may observe the final construction of the merchant group.[58]

Several counter-examples show a dampening influence of kinship on economic activity. David Landes has argued that the peculiar structure of the French business family has kept the typical firm small and thus inhibited economic growth. Specific features of family life are the refusal to go outside the family circle for acquiring capital (for this would mean a loss of exclusiveness), a hesitation to separate family budgeting from business budgeting (which impedes rational bookkeeping), and recruitment into the firm on grounds other than business ability.[59] In his study of the Chinese family, Marion Levy isolated the factors of particularistic favoritism and functional diffuseness as characteristics of Chinese kinship that constituted barriers to industrialization.[60]

From these cases we conclude that kinship sometimes encourages and sometimes discourages certain economic activities. But we need to know the conditions under which a given type of kinship structure will facilitate or obstruct a given type of economic activity. This requires a systematic typology of kinship structures, a systematic typology of economic structures, a statement of conditions and controls to which both types of structures are subject, and a vast body of comparative research.

Much recent literature on the family as a dependent variable *vis à vis* the economic activity of a society has centered on a single question: What has been the impact of industrialization on the modern family, especially the American family? This question, like that concerning the dominant political influences in modern American society, is shot through with confusion and controversy.

One school of thought argues that the American family has deteriorated under the impact of urban industrial life. Reasons for this position include the increase of divorce in the West during the past century, the decline of parental authority, the decline of deep emotional relations between the spouses, the deleterious effects of unemployment on family

[56] James C. Abegglen, "Subordination and Autonomy Attitudes of Japanese Workers," *American Journal of Sociology* (1957–1958), 63: 181–189.
[57] Arensberg and Kimball, *op. cit.*, Chapters VI, VIII.
[58] "Kinship and Trade in Seventeenth Century New England," *Explorations in Entrepreneurial History* (May 1954), 6: 197–206.
[59] "French Business and the Businessman: A Social and Cultural Analysis," in E. M. Earle (ed.), *Modern France* (Princeton: Princeton University Press, 1951), pp. 334–353.
[60] *The Family Revolution in Modern China* (Cambridge: Harvard University Press, 1949), pp. 350–365.

life, and the rise of delinquency. All these, it is commonly asserted, are signs of deterioration; this deterioration, moreover, is intimately associated with the encroachments of the urban-industrial way of life.[61]

There are two alternative formulations to this thesis. The first, associated with the name of Talcott Parsons, argues that while it is true that the modern American family has undergone fundamental changes—indeed, changes connected with urbanization and industrialization—it is erroneous to refer to these familial changes in terms of "disorganization." Rather, the family has become a more specialized kind of structure in several senses. True, the family has lost *some* of its functions (such as producing economic goods and services as a cooperative unit, educating its children at formal levels); but it has become the more exclusive guardian of other functions (specifically, socializing the very young child and providing a setting for emotional tension-management for adults). In addition, the roles of the husband-father and wife-mother have become more specialized relative to one another. That is, the man has become the more exclusive performer of the "instrumental" (external, income-generating) functions of the family, the woman of the "expressive" (social-emotional) functions. These new structural features of the family, Parsons argues, signify the opposite of disintegration; they show a nuclear family that is more effective than its predecessor in socializing children for adult roles in a modern urban-industrial complex.[62]

The other alternative formulation is that the family has not changed as radically as argued in the "pessimistic" approach. Eugene Litwak has suggested that while the demands of the modern occupational structure make for high family mobility, this has not destroyed the extended family. In fact, Litwak asserts that "because technological improvements in communication systems have minimized the socially disruptive forces of geographical distance, and because an extended family can provide important aid to nuclear families without interfering with the occupational system," a sort of "modified extended family" has survived into the mid-twentieth century. Litwak attempts to buttress his assertions with studies of visiting patterns in large cities.[63]

In sum, we are unable definitely to assess the exact impact of urban-industrial life on the family. At present, we can settle only for a period of competition among assertions about very general trends.

An analysis of family structure does illuminate two important economic phenomena—the problem of female participation in the labor force and the problem of the aged. In general, women display a higher turnover rate in employment than men; they enter casual and temporary employment more frequently; they cluster disproportionately in occupations such as nursing, teaching, and secretarial and clerical work. Furthermore, their level of participation is closely associated with age and marital status. A

---

[61] For variants on the position, see W. F. Ogburn, "The Family and Its Functions," in Presidents' Research Committee on Social Trends, *Recent Social Trends in the United States* (New York: McGraw-Hill, 1933); Ernest W. Burgess and Harvey J. Locke, *The Family* (New York: American Book, 1950).

[62] Talcott Parsons, Robert F. Bales, *et al.*, *Family, Socialization and Interaction Process* (Glencoe, Ill.: The Free Press, 1955), Chapter I.

[63] "Occupational Mobility and Extended Family Cohesion," and "Geographic Mobility and Extended Family Cohesion," *American Sociological Review* (1960), 25: 9–21, 385–394.

high participation rate is evident in the late 'teens and early twenties. A severe drop in participation characterizes the child-bearing years, but about age 30 the rate of participation begins to climb rapidly again.[64]

Clearly these features of female employment are largely a function of the contemporary American family structure. Because of the woman's primary responsibility for young children, her participation rate slumps in these years. Because she is subject to the demands of home, and because she is absent from the labor market for a number of years, she cannot pursue a straight career line as easily as can a man; hence the tendency to enter part-time, less enduring employment. In addition, the long-term upward trend in female labor-force participation may be related to the fact that the family has lost some of its educational functions to nursery schools and schools. During the years that these structures "take over" responsibility for the children, women have become "free" to enter employment outside the home. Finally, since women enter quasi-maternal and supportive occu-pations (nursing, teaching, social welfare, secretarial-clerical), a continuity exists between familial and occupational roles.[65]

With the increasing life expectancy associated with the development of modern medicine, combined with the institutionalization of retirement, the problem of the unemployed aged has become increasingly severe. Not only are the unemployed aged (especially widows) subject to economic deprivation, but they are often victims of painful adjustments to isolation and loss of identity.[66]

The isolation of the aged is in part a function of the kinship organi-zation of the modern Western world. One of the broad trends in the development of the urban-industrial family is its increasing mobility and its tendency to be mobile as a two-generation unit—parents and their young children. Oldsters are left behind; they no longer have a distinctive kinship role.[67] This contrasts with more traditional family structures, in which the aged continued to have a meaningful role, sometimes highly venerated. In such systems of kinship, social security and "medical care for the aged" are less necessary. The need for such welfare measures for the aged, then, reflects not only the economic status of the aged, but the absence of significant membership in a kinship unit that will be responsible for care and sustenance of its aged.

[64] For data on these regularities, cf. National Manpower Council, *Womanpower* (New York: Columbia University Press, 1957), pp. 65–70, 125–135, and 241–250; Thomas A. Mahoney, "Factors Determining the Labor-Force Participation of Married Women," *Industrial and Labor Relations Review* (1960–1961), 14: 563–577; Harold L. Wilensky, "Work, Careers, and Social Integration," *International Social Science Journal* (1960), 12: 543–560.

[65] Even in the medical profession, women doctors tend to specialize in pediatrics, child psychiatry, and other specialties associated with the welfare of children.

[66] Philip M. Hauser, "Changes in the Labor-Force Participation of the Older Worker," *American Journal of Sociology* (1953–1954), 59: 312–323; Peter O. Steiner and Robert Dorfman, *The Economic Status of the Aged* (Berkeley and Los Angeles: University of California Press, 1957), pp. 1–66, 146–152. One of several attitudinal studies of the aged about retirement is found in Eugene A. Friedmann and Robert J. Havighurst, *et al., The Meaning of Work and Retirement* (Chicago: University of Chicago Press, 1954).

[67] We should not underplay, however, the widespread use of grandmothers and other older women in the care of the young children of the wife who works or who is otherwise occupied.

61

History provides many instances of the fusion between membership in an ethnic group and membership in an economic role. Perhaps the most familiar is that found in the pattern of American immigration. Roughly speaking, migrants throughout the past 150 years have filled the lowest economic rung—unskilled labor—upon arrival, only to be displaced "upward" by the new waves. A striking example of these waves of ethnic succession is found in the agricultural labor market in California:

> The Chinese have disappeared. The Japanese, once prominent, have for the most part moved into some type of land proprietorship, or into commercial occupations. . . . The great bulk of the casual work force in agriculture is Mexican and native white. In certain crops, notably asparagus and lettuce, the Filipino is prominent. Since the war Negroes, originally attracted by the shipyards and aircraft factories as much as by cotton, have become increasingly important in the seasonal agricultural labor force.[68]

Although ethnic groups in the United States have remained at the very lowest economic rung for only a short time, they have moved upward economically at different rates. Four factors determine the relative speed of ascent:

1. *Economic conditions of demand.* The rise of the Negro during World War II and the postwar prosperity has resulted in large part from increased economic opportunities throughout the occupational structure.

2. *The internal resources of the ethnic group itself, both financial and socio-cultural.* Thus the Jews, Greeks and Armenians, with a much more highly developed commercial tradition than the Polish, Irish, or Italian peasant, possessed an initial advantage in terms of capital and commercial skills. Also, the pattern of kinship and community loyalties of the Irish male fitted him particularly for the talents required in American political party life, in which the Irish have been notably successful.

3. *The continuing strength of particularistic ties.* Once an inroad on a new, higher-level occupational rung is made by a given ethnic group, the successful few will allocate their new talent and resources to "bring in" people of their own kind to reap the advantages. This particularistic pressure applies in varying degree to every ethnic group.

4. *The degree to which the ethnic group is "held back" through discrimination by the majority group.* Every ethnic minority has experienced some discrimination; but for the Negro this has been most extreme. Hence the Negro is consigned to the ranks of manual labor and servant work, and is underrepresented in professional, business, and clerical occupations.[69]

Discrimination rests on two bases—direct, in which employers resist employment of Negroes because they are Negroes; and indirect, when

---

[68] Fisher, *op. cit.*, p. 6.

[69] St. Clair Drake and Horace R. Cayton, *Black Metropolis* (New York: Harcourt, Brace, 1945), pp. 214 ff.; Donald Dewey, "Negro Employment in Southern Industry," *Journal of Political Economy* (1952), 60: 279–293; for an account of Negro advances in the acquisition of property during the past century, cf. E. Franklin Frazier, *Black Bourgeoisie* (Glencoe, Ill.: The Free Press, 1957), pp. 29–51.

employers refuse to hire Negroes because they are less technically qualified for employment—which usually means that they have experienced discrimination elsewhere in the system, especially in education.

However, in the United States no single ethnic group has been permanently attached to a particular economic role (though some ethnic groups do dominate certain industries, such as the Armenians in the rug industry). In some colonial societies a somewhat more fixed relationship between ethnic membership and other roles has emerged. In many Asian and African colonies, the social order broke more or less imperfectly into three groupings: first, the Western representatives (British, French, or Dutch, e.g.) who controlled the larger economic enterprises and political administration, and who frequently were allied with powerful local landowners; second, a large native population who—when drawn into the colonial economy—entered as tenant farmers, wage laborers, and the like; and third, a group of foreigners—Chinese, Indians, Syrians, Goans, Lebanese—who fitted "in between" the first two as traders, money-lenders, merchants, creditors, and so on. The important structural feature of such a system is that economic, political, and racial-ethnic memberships *coincide* with one another.

One consequence of this coincidence of ethnic and other cleavages is that *any* kind of conflict (e.g., economic competition) is likely to assume racial overtones and arouse the more diffuse loyalties and prejudices of the warring parties. Conflict thus generalizes to a much more disruptive level because it involves not merely conflicts of interest but also conflicts of values and "ways of life." Many outbursts in colonial societies did in fact follow racial lines.[70] Or to take another set of examples, British coal-miners' opposition to imported Polish, Italian, and Hungarian labor was considerably inflamed because they were foreign groups.[71] On the side of the minority group, too, diffuse hostility can develop when group memberships and economic roles coincide. One interesting complication arising from the development of a business community among the Negroes in cities like Chicago—a development accompanied by a "rise of a Negro business spirit and Negro business chauvinism"—is the appearance of sometimes considerable anti-Semitism among the Negroes, who feel themselves in immediate and keen competition with Jewish merchants.[72] Such are the types of generalized conflicts that are likely to arise when ethnic-racial and other structures coincide. If, on the other hand, the various lines of social cleavage cut across one another, specific economic and political grievances are more peacefully managed.

A final point is in order with respect to the economic influence of ethnic membership. Ethnic groups generally impose sanctions on their members to interact *within* the group with relatively greater frequency than they interact *outside* the group. There is pressure to vote for one's own kind, to marry one's own kind, and so on. We might suggest that the intensity of economic interaction within ethnic groups is directly related

[70] Rupert Emerson, Lennox A. Mills, and Virginia Thompson, *Government and Nationalism in Southeast Asia* (New York: Institute of Pacific Relations, 1942), pp. 141–143; Erich H. Jacoby, *Agrarian Unrest in Southeast Asia* (New York: Columbia University Press, 1949), Chapter VIII.

[71] Baldwin, *op. cit.*, pp. 194–199.

[72] Harold L. Sheppard, "The Negro Merchant: A Study of Negro Anti-Semitism," *American Journal of Sociology* (1947–1948), 53: 96–99

to the degree of knowledge of market conditions.[73] To illustrate: In an analysis of the spatial distribution of physicians in Chicago, Stanley Lieberson found that doctors of a certain ethnic background (Jewish or Irish, e.g.) tended to concentrate and practice in the corresponding ethnic area of the city. Those ethnic groups that were overrepresented among physicians (Jews, Anglo-Saxons) tended to concentrate in the Loop area and to concentrate in the medical specializations.[74] This ethnic association between occupational role and recipients of services is greater in medicine than it is in retail food distribution, pharmacies, and so on. The reason for this is that medical practice is, for most patients, both an "unknown" product (we cannot know its quality by trying it on or tasting it) *and* a product about which people have extremely deep emotional feelings. Because of these obstacles to economic calculation, people fall back on new criteria for choosing services; they go to people "of their own kind" whom they feel they can trust. Often these people turn out to be members of their own ethnic group. The implications of this reasoning for the analysis of imperfect competition is that in the absence of knowledge or emotional neutrality about a product, people will fall back on solidary groupings when purchasing goods and services. This criterion forms one of the key bases on which markets deviate from the perfectly competitive model.

Social Stratification and Economic Life

Above we cited research that indicated a strain toward consistency between types of economic system and types of family structure. These same extensive patterns of structural coherence are evident in the relations between economic arrangements and stratification systems. Arthur Stinchcombe has related typical agricultural enterprises with typical patterns of stratification and styles of life.[75]

Type of Enterprise	Characteristics of Enterprise	Characteristics of Class Structure
Manorial	Division of land into domain land and labor subsistence land, with domain land devoted to production for market. Technology traditional; low cost of land and little market in land.	Classes differ greatly in legal privileges and style of life. Technical culture borne largely by the peasantry.
Family-size tenancy	Small parcels of highly valuable land worked by families who do not own the land, with a large share of the production for market. Highly labor- and land-intensive culture, of yearly or more frequent crops.	Classes differ little in legal privileges but greatly in style of life. Technical culture generally borne by the lower classes.

[73] The model of perfect competition, it will be recalled, posited complete knowledge of market conditions for all actors.

[74] "Ethnic Groups and the Practice of Medicine," *American Sociological Review* (1958), 23: 542–549.

[75] "Agricultural Enterprise and Rural Class Relations," *American Journal of Sociology* (1961–1962), 67: 165–176.

the economy and other social sub-systems

Type of Enterprise	Characteristics of Enterprise	Characteristics of Class Structure
Family small-holding	Same as family tenancy, except benefits remain within the enterprise . . . may become capital-intensive at a late stage of industrialization.	Classes differ neither in legal privileges nor in style of life. Technical culture borne by rich and poor.
Plantation	Large-scale enterprises with either slavery or wage labor, producing labor-intensive crops requiring capital investment on relatively cheap land. . . . No or little subsistence production.	Classes differ in both style of life and legal privileges. Technical culture monopolized by upper classes.
Ranch	Large-scale production of labor-extensive crops, on land of low value, with wage labor partly paid in kind in company barracks and mess.	Classes may not differ in legal status, as there is no need to recruit and keep down a large labor force. Style of life differences unknown. Technically culture generally relatively evenly distributed.

Such structural coherence between economic structures and types of stratification appears in industrial societies as well. Alex Inkeles and Peter Rossi found that occupations associated with industrial production (engineer, foreman, machine worker, etc.) were assigned very similar positions in the general prestige hierarchy of occupations of a number of industrialized nations. In fact, the over-all similarity of the occupational prestige hierarchies among these nations traced largely to the parallel rankings of industrial occupations.[76] It is important, however, not to overemphasize the identity of prestige stratification in industrial societies. Inkeles and Rossi found, for instance, that occupations not inherently associated with industrialization—clergyman, military officer, doctor—differed greatly in prestige among industrialized societies.

Another broad structural congruence is between type of stratification system and type of social and economic mobility. By mobility we refer to the movement of persons through the economic hierarchy. This mobility may take two forms: (1) The movement of *individuals* through a hierarchy of positions. In the traditional American ideology this type of mobility is emphasized. (2) The movement of *groups* of *organizations* through a hierarchy of positions. The most common form of this type of mobility is the movement of family units, as when the head of the household advances through the occupational hierarchy, and the status of his dependent family members moves along with his. Another form of this mobility is the movement of formal organizations, as when an academic department, by great effort, "breaks into" the ranks of top-ranking departments.

One of the major determinants of the form of mobility—individual

[76] "National Comparisons of Occupational Prestige," *American Journal of Sociology* (1956–1957), 61: 329–339.

or collective—is found in the degree to which a stratification system is based on ascription or achievement. Societies vary considerably in the degree to which roles (occupational, religious, political) follow from status ascribed at birth. The basis of ascription may be kinship, age, sex, race or ethnicity, or territorial location. Insofar as these criteria constitute the basis for entering roles, the society emphasizes ascription. Insofar as admission is independent of ascribed bases and rests on some sort of behavior performance on the part of persons, the society emphasizes achievement.

The implications of the ascription-achievement dimension for the typical form of the social mobility in a society is as follows: If ascription is firmly institutionalized, mobility tends to be collective; if achievement is firmly institutionalized, mobility tends to be individual.

To illustrate: A stratification system at the ascriptive extreme is to be found in classical India. Typically, the individual was born into a caste, and virtually every aspect of future life was determined by this membership—his marriage choice, his occupation, his associational memberships, his ritual behavior, his type of funeral. Choices were made for him from the instant of birth. Because roles were settled in this way, individual mobility from caste to caste was impossible in the lifetime of one individual. The structure of the caste system did not permit it. What form did mobility take in such a system? According to Hutton's account, mobility manifested itself as the *collective* splitting off of sub-castes, or what he calls the "fissiparous tendencies in Indian castes." He refers to a process whereby a caste was segregated into a sub-caste, which for a time accepted wives from other sub-castes but simultaneously refused to give daughters to these sub-castes. This established a claim to superiority, which was fortified by some change in occupational duties. The final step was to adopt a new caste name and deny all connection with the caste of origin. Thus, in Hutton's language, "by organization and propaganda a caste can change its name and in the course of time get a new one accepted, and by altering its canons of behavior in the matter of diet and marriage can increase the estimation in which it is held." [77] This multiplication of castes over the centuries is the clue to the distinctive form of mobility in classical India.

A stratification system at the achievement extreme is found in the traditional American system. This system encourages the movement of individual persons away from ascribed positions (based on region, ethnic background, even family orientation) into new roles. In practice, of course, ascribed characteristics, especially racial ones, prevent the operation of this system in pure form.

One reason why hostility toward "welfare" practices in the United States is pronounced lies in this distinctive American emphasis on achievement. The introduction of welfare measures means bringing facilities and rewards to certain defined classes of persons, rather than having persons work their way to these facilities and rewards. One of the interesting justifications for introducing welfare measures in the United States—as opposed to continental European states, where state welfare is taken more for granted—is that such measures must presumably *facilitate* equality of opportunity for individuals in the society. If it can be argued that *not* to give welfare somehow impedes the life chances of a potentially mobile

[77] J. H. Hutton, *Caste in India* (Cambridge: Cambridge University Press, 1946), pp. 41–61, 97–100.

the economy and other social sub-systems

individual or class of individuals, then welfare measures are more likely to be judged legitimate.

Within the United States some interesting variations on the predominantly individual form of mobility are observable. When a person assumes an adult occupational role and reaches, say, age 30, his mobility as an individual is more or less completed, except perhaps within the same occupational category. Thus adults holding the same occupational status are in certain respects in ascribed positions, though this ascription is not a matter of their position at birth. Under these circumstances mobility tends to become collective. Entire occupational groups (nurses, for instance) try to improve their position, or to safeguard it from erosion. Collective mobility in the American system becomes legitimate, in short, when the battle for individual mobility comes to an effective close for the individual, and when he becomes lodged in an ascribed group.

Thus the *form* of mobility is closely related to the structure of the stratification system. In addition, the *rate* of upward mobility is closely related to the type of economic system. According to studies conducted by Seymour M. Lipset and Reinhard Bendix, "the overall pattern [rates] of social mobility appears to be much the same in the industrial societies of various Western countries." [78] This runs counter to the common assumption that the United States is a relatively "open" society by contrast with many of the more traditional Western countries. Lipset and Bendix maintain that it is not the ideological and cultural differences among countries that influence rates of mobility most of all, but rather similarities and differences in their occupational structures. Thus industrial societies will present broad over-all similarities in rates of mobility.

Lipset and Bendix' findings must be tempered by two qualifications. First, not all the Western societies they studied—the United States, Sweden, France, Italy, Finland, for instance—are to the same degree industrialized nor have they changed at the same rates. Thus factors other than industrial experience make for such striking similarities in the rates of mobility. Second, the only major type of mobility index utilized in Lipset and Bendix' comparative analysis was the movement from manual to non-manual occupations. This index, while helpful for some purposes, is so gross as to conceal many sources of meaningful variation, such as the movement from business into professional occupations.

One of the widely discussed topics in contemporary American sociology concerns the present state of the American class system. The most vocal side of the discussions—coming in varied ways from the late C. Wright Mills, Peter Drucker, W. Lloyd Warner, and Vance Packard—asserts that the American stratification system is "hardening," becoming less "open" to opportunity, or even that people are becoming less motivated to move upward.[79] Among the most obvious reasons for inferring such a decline in upward mobility are the facts that foreign migration—which supplied a "floor" of unskilled labor—diminished as a result of the

[78] *Social Mobility in Industrial Society* (Berkeley and Los Angeles: University of California Press, 1959), p. 13.

[79] C. Wright Mills, *White Collar* (New York: Oxford University Press, 1951), p. 259; Peter F. Drucker, "The Employee Society," *American Journal of Sociology*, (1952–1953), 58: 358–363; W. Lloyd Warner and J. O. Low, *The Social System of the Modern Factory* (New Haven: Yale University Press, 1947), p. 185; Vance Packard, *The Status Seekers* (New York: McKay, 1959).

immigration laws of the 1920's; that the differential birth rates between classes have been diminishing gradually for many decades; that many studies showing inflexibilities in mobility have been conducted in local communities (where mobility to other communities is seldom measured); and that many of the studies of stratification in such communities were conducted in the stagnant depression period of the 1930's.

While a great deal of research on inter-generational mobility, the origin of elites, and career mobility is being conducted in American sociology,[80] the discussion of the current state of American social stratification yields much more heat than light. In this sense the discussion resembles those concerning the contemporary state of the American power structure and the American family.[81] Most research on the long-term trends in rates of mobility indicates very little if any change over the past half-century, except perhaps for a very slightly upward trend which was slowed perceptibly by the depression of the 1930's.[82]

Conclusion

The continuous theme in this chapter has been the relations between economic and non-economic variables at the level of society as a whole. Now we change lenses. We shall continue to focus on the relations between economic and non-economic variables, but we shall do so at the more microscopic level of economic processes.

[80] Summaries of such research are found in Natalie Rogoff, *Recent Trends in Occupational Mobility* (Glencoe, Ill.: The Free Press, 1953), pp. 19–28; W. Lloyd Warner and James C. Abegglen, *Occupational Mobility in American Business and Industry* (Minneapolis: University of Minnesota Press, 1955), pp. 13–25; Lipset and Bendix, *op. cit.*

[81] Above, pp. 56–57, 59–60.

[82] Examples of the most careful research are found in Rogoff, *op. cit.*; Sidney Goldstein, "Migration and Occupational Mobility in Norristown, Pennsylvania," *American Sociological Review* (1955), 20: 402–403; Stuart Adams, "Origins of American Occupational Elites, 1900–1955," *American Journal of Sociology* (1956–1957), 62: 360–368.

sociological
analysis
of economic
processes
four

Economists commonly view the economic process as one of *production* and *consumption*. Production involves the assembling and applying of resources; consumption, the "using up" of the resultant product. Unlike consumption, production does not involve satisfaction of human wants. The process of production and consumption necessitates some technique for *distribution*—i.e., channeling inputs (raw materials, capital, and labor) to the firm, and outputs to the consumers.[1]

In this chapter we shall use this view of the economic process as an organizing principle. First, we shall observe the sociological variables that impinge on production. Second, we shall investigate distribution and exchange, in particular the implications of different structural arrangements for exchange itself, and the intervention of sociological variables on the markets for labor services, entrepreneurial services, and consumer's goods. Third, we shall turn to consumption, assembling some disparate results of research that has been accumulating in economics and sociology.

[1] The market for services (e.g., those of a refrigerator repairman) "compresses" the markets for inputs and outputs in a certain sense, for such services are simultaneously a factor of production (in the production of chilled food) and a commodity consumed by the household.

The Production Process

Technical Determinants

Marx distinguished between the forces of production and the social relations of production.[2] The former refer to the relations among tools, time, and tasks that arise by virtue of the concrete technical features of the work situation. An example of the forces of production would be the demands imposed on men by an automatic machine in a factory—demands that certain workers gear their own work pace to the motions of the machine, that other workers clean and repair the machine from time to time, and so on. The social relations of production refer to those human interactions that arise when men engage in production. Examples of social relations would be the division of human labor into specialized and interdependent work roles, into authority relations, and so on. The development of social relations does not stop with the interactions necessary to complete the process of production. By virtue of close and continuous association, new forms—friendships, cliques, prestige systems—arise.

Marx believed the social relations of production to be dependent on the social forces of production. In this chapter we shall not adhere to this view. We shall show how social relations feed back into the productive process. First, however, we shall mention some of the technical determinants of social relations in productive contexts.

By "technical determinants" we refer to certain physical and biological factors associated with the concrete productive process; these include "size of the plant and company; seasonal and cyclical stability of its production pattern; volume, nature, rate of technical change," illumination and noise at the workplace, and the biological limitations on the workers.[3]

These technical determinants affect human activities and interaction in the following ways:

1. The technical arrangements of work determine in large part the degree of physical exertion required from the organism. In the past several decades investigators of fatigue and productivity have studied the significance of temperature, rest pauses, length of work day and work week.[4] The results of these studies are difficult to assess, largely because such factors are so contaminated by social and psychological variables.

2. Technical features of the job influence the pacing of work. This is most conspicuous in assembly-line work.

3. Technical arrangements of production influence the level of skill required of workers. A familiar example is the difference in skill level between the craftsman—sometimes requiring years of apprenticeship—and the assembly-line worker—whose skills are elementary and can be learned within a matter of minutes or hours. The loss of skills which resulted from industrialization is a basic cause of the lack of identification with the product often attributed to industrial workers.

[2] Above, p. 7.

[3] Abraham J. Siegel, "The Economic Environment in Human Relations Research," in Conrad M. Arensberg, *et al.* (eds.), *Research in Industrial Human Relations: A Critical Appraisal* (New York: Harper, 1957), p. 89; for a brief account of the research on the effect of illumination and noise on productivity, cf. Wilbert E. Moore, *Industrial Relations and the Social Order*, rev. ed. (New York: Macmillan, 1951), p. 217.

[4] Part of this research is summarized in Moore, *op. cit.*, pp. 211–217.

sociological analysis of economic processes

4. Technical features determine the degree of complexity of the division of labor. Modern industry has carried worker specialization to a level never before reached in human history.

5. Most important for the study of economic sociology, technical features of work influence the character of social interaction. The physical pattern of work calls for certain kinds of cooperation, communication, and authority on the job. This influence often extends to off-the-job interaction as well. A salient feature of modern family life is that for most of the daylight hours one or more family members are absent in a workplace. Or, to choose a more striking example, the timing of work invades almost every aspect of the life of a railroader:

> . . . the pattern of social relationships set by the occupation vitally affects the social life of the railroader. It prevents normal relationships between wife and husband, father and child. While cutting him off from most other group behavior, thus intensifying their significance, these time relationships also interfere with normal family group activities such as eating, sleeping, and recreation. Time-dependency cuts the family off from other groups in the community as well as its members from each other. It interferes with community activity, preventing the assumption of civic responsibility, and denying status so gained.[5]

The introduction of automation in recent years has stirred up an interest in the social consequences of the technical features of production. Strictly speaking, almost all industrial advance has meant "automation" in the sense that low-level skills have been taken over by the automatic operation of machines. The distinctive character of automation in the mid-twentieth century involves continuous production of commodities that are not touched by human hands; moreover, modern automation has mechanized a much higher level of skills, particularly those connected with computer control and the use of feedback mechanisms.[6]

1. By contrast with the assembly line, the automated factory will lessen the amount of physical labor required by workmen and will shorten the work day and work week. In most cases automation will reduce the number of workers in the factory, though its long-term effect on employment levels is uncertain.[7]

2. The pacing of work will be removed even further from the control of workmen than under assembly-line production.

3. The level of skill will be upgraded. A whole range of unskilled and semi-skilled positions (repairmen, clerks, typists) will be wiped out. Technicians will have to be more highly educated and trained than ever before. Engineers will multiply.[8]

4. At the lower levels, automation will reduce specialization by removing personnel and positions. At the higher skill levels new specializations, demanding more detailed knowledge and training, will proliferate.

[5] W. Fred Cottrell, *The Railroader* (Stanford: Stanford University Press, 1940), pp. 76–77.

[6] Michel Crozier and Georges Friedmann, "Forward," to "The Social Consequences of Automation," *International Social Science Bulletin* (1958), 10: 7–8.

[7] Frederick Pollock, *Automation: A Study of its Economic and Social Consequences* (New York: Praeger, 1957), pp. 203–212; Floyd C. Mann and L. Richard Hoffman, "Individual and Organizational Correlates of Automation," *Journal of Social Issues* (1957), 12: 11.

[8] Pollock, *op. cit.*, pp. 212–217.

5. The effects of automation on social relations on the job are not clear. In an investigation of an automated power plant, Floyd Mann and Richard Hoffman found a reduction in the degree of physical isolation of the workers.[9] In a study of an automated automobile plant, however, William Faunce found significantly less interaction among working groups, smaller interaction groups, more contact with foremen, and more contact with superintendent—in short more isolation from peers—than the workers recalled from their previous non-automated jobs.[10]

Because automated industry requires highly-skilled workmen and engineers in large proportions, one possible impact on a community dominated by an automated industry will be an uplifting of the educational level of its citizenry. This will probably affect patterns of civic participation, governmental processes, and entertainment patterns in the community.

As Faunce points out, the introduction of automation may reduce the importance of many variables stressed heavily in modern industrial sociology. As we shall see below, many modern investigations focus on the impact of variables (such as the quality of supervision and the character of informal work groups) on morale and the corresponding impact of morale on worker productivity. Many of these determinants disappear in the automated setting. The morale of work groups has less immediate effect on output, because the machines are controlled automatically in so many respects; nor can the foreman, traditionally a pivotal figure in morale and productivity, influence the level of output in an immediate sense. On the basis of such observations, Faunce has called for a reassessment of the significance of the work group in industry.[11]

In this introductory section we have considered the social aspect of work as dependent on the technical features of the work situation. Now we shall treat this social aspect as a subject in its own right. We shall apply the general variables of economic sociology to the social relations of production; we shall observe how the social aspects feed back into the technical features.

For purposes of analysis we shall divide the social aspect of production into two basic units of social structure—*occupational roles* and *organizations*. Roles and organizations overlap in two ways. First, sometimes an individual in a role (for instance, an individual medical practitioner) faces all the essential problems of production and distribution, and thus is a sort of "one man organization." Second, organizations consist of an interlocking set of roles (engineers, foreman, workmen, etc.).

Occupational Roles

Economists' versions of the attitudes and behavior of persons in occupational roles follow the logic of supply and demand. They assume that the amount of work offered by an individual in the market is some function of the economic rewards available to him. The prototypical supply curve would thus be smooth and upward-sloping:

[9] *Op. cit.*, p. 14.
[10] "Automation in the Automobile Industry: Some Consequences for In-Plant Social Structure," *American Sociological Review* (1958), 23: 403–406.
[11] *Ibid.*, pp. 406–407.

sociological analysis of economic processes

Quantity of labor

At times economists have reconsidered this simple notion. Thus Keynes argued that, while the general relation between wages and labor is positive, the individual chooses to withdraw his labor altogether from the market rather than merely work less if wages are lowered beyond a certain level:

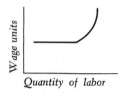

Quantity of labor

This assumption plays an important role in Keynes' account of the level of unemployment in his equilibrium system. Other economists have stressed that particularly in economically underdeveloped areas wage increases will bring forth not more but less labor, because the individual prefers to spend his additional earnings on leisure activities rather than to work more. This produces a backward-sloping supply curve: [12]

Quantity of labor

Finally, economists allow for the possibility that under certain conditions —for instance, changes in value systems, changes in technology—a labor supply curve may shift to the right or left.

From the standpoint of economic sociology, economists' notions on role behavior display the following limitations:

1. Such views ignore the mutual interdependence among laborers. This objection constitutes one of the main attacks by industrial sociologists on economists:

> [Many managers and social science investigators adhere to] the belief that an industrial organization is an aggregation of individuals, each seeking his own gain without reference to other persons, and consequently each capable of being induced to greater effort by devices focused upon

---

[12] For a critical view of the notion of a backward-sloping curve, even for the underdeveloped areas, cf. Harold G. Vatter, "On the Folklore of the Backward-Sloping Supply Curve," *Industrial and Labor Relations Review* (1960–1961), 14: 578–586.

this desire for advantage. To this assumption [Elton] Mayo opposes the view that a working force normally consists of social groups, whose members are highly responsive to each other's social gestures and identify their fates with those of their fellows; social groups which, further, are related to others in the larger system of social relations in and about industry.[13]

2. Even though economists acknowledge that social factors (such as extended kinship obligations or traditional religious beliefs) influence a labor-supply curve, perhaps in a backward-sloping direction, they assume these social factors to be "given." While permissible for purposes of formal economic analysis, this assumption is not sufficient for economic sociologists, who aim to investigate *systematically* the factors themselves.

3. In practice the positive functional relation between wages and labor does not seem to work out, as seen in the ineffectiveness and even backfiring of incentive schemes such as piecework and merit schemes.[14]

4. The economic sociologist would insist that many more variables than wages alone determine changes in the amount of work offered by a laborer. To mention only one such variable, the kind and amount of supervision influences the effort put forth on the job. In addition, the economic sociologist is interested in types of behavior other than the amount of labor expended; he focuses on ideologies of the worker, his interactions with other workers, his responses to authority, and so on. In short, the economic sociologist expands the number of dependent and independent variables beyond the scope envisioned by the economist. This expansion gives him both a strength and a weakness; he is better able to make the behavior of individual workers more meaningful, but he is less able to organize his more complex subject-matter into a theoretically adequate framework.

The sociologist's conception of role (of which occupational role is one type) refers to an organized cluster of *activities* involving *interaction* with the physical, social, and cultural environments. These activities are structured and regulated by *expectations*. "Expectations" means more than predictability of behavior; it also means that definite *norms* and *sanctions* are brought to bear to induce the role incumbent to conform to standards of conduct. Among the sanctions, economic rewards and deprivations are important, but they are only one of several available sanctions.

Given these concepts by which role behavior is described, sociologists often proceed to identify certain types of *strains* that typically arise in roles. Above we outlined several kinds of strains—ambiguity, deprivation, norm-conflict, and value-conflict. In addition, we considered certain *reactions to strain* that lead to attitudinal changes (e.g., lowered morale, adherence to a magical belief or ideological position) and behavioral changes (e.g., lowered productivity, absenteeism).[15]

[13] Summarized in Everett Cherrington Hughes, "The Knitting of Racial Groups in Industry," *American Sociological Review* (1946), 2: 512. Some economists have attempted to assess the influence of labor unions on labor supply curves; see, for instance, John T. Dunlop, *Wage Determination under Trade Unions* (New York: Augustus M. Kelley, 1950), pp. 28–44.

[14] For summaries of the literature on these incentive schemes, cf. Burleigh B. Gardner and David G. Moore, *Human Relations in Industry*, 3rd ed. (Homewood, Ill.: Irwin, 1955), pp. 189–204; Morris S. Viteles, *Motivation and Morale in Industry* (New York: Norton, 1953), pp. 127 ff.

[15] Above, pp. 29–30.

74

So much for the comparison and contrast between economic and sociological approaches to role behavior. Let us now consider several of the occupational roles that have been analyzed in recent sociological literature:

The Executive Role.

As the business corporation has grown more complex in recent American history, the executive or top managerial roles have taken on new dimensions. Traditionally, the model of personal profit-maximization was inseparable from the notion of the businessman. That is to say, if he made the correct decisions regarding the allocation of resources, he would receive the profits. By mid-twentieth century the relation between businessmen and profits has become more complex. Profits of the firm still reflect the correctness of his decisions. However, because of the split between ownership and executive control, a very large share of these profits accrue not directly to him but to stockholders less actively involved in decision-making. Even with bonuses and promotions for effective management the model of *direct* profit-maximization is not realized. If the modern executive is not a profit-maximizer in the classical sense, then, what are his functions?

Basically, the modern executive role focuses on the political and integrative features of the business firm. Clearly the executive's primary responsibility is decision-making at the policy level; on the basis of his decisions the various departments of the firm—budgeting, personnel, sales —presumably carry out his policies. In addition, the executive is a coordinator—he must see that things get done on time, be a "trouble-shooter," listen to grievances and problems of heads of departments, and so on. With regard to the firm's external relations as well, many of his activities are coordinative—to balance off the demands of consumers, bankers, stockholders, directors, union leaders, and so on.[16]

Sociologists have identified typical strains in the executive's role: (1) He is under pressure to come to responsible decisions in a relatively brief time, despite the fact that many decisions must be made in a situation of ambiguity or uncertainty. The businessman simply does not know all the facts about his firm and its market situation; even if he knows them, he cannot be certain they will be the same in the near future. (2) His role demands an impersonality in his human relations. Because of the institutionalization of the standards of calculation, profit-making, responsibility, and authority, the businessman must be practical and sometimes even ruthless in his dealing with human beings. He sometimes has to issue unpleasant orders; he is often under pressure to fire incompetent subordinates, even though they might in other contexts be his friends.[17]

The corresponding reactions to strain in the executive role are as follows:

[16] Chester I. Barnard, *The Functions of the Executive* (Cambridge: Harvard University Press, 1958); also his "The Nature of Leadership," in Barnard, *Organization and Management* (Cambridge: Harvard University Press, 1956), pp. 80–110; also Robert A. Gordon, *Business Leadership in the Large Corporation* (Washington, D. C.: Brookings Institution, 1945).

[17] For discussion of these and other strains in the businessman's role, cf. Sutton, *et al.*, *The American Business Creed* (Cambridge: Harvard University Press, 1956), Chap. 16; Eugene V. Schneider and Sverre Lysgaard, *Industrial Sociology* (New York: McGraw-Hill, 1957), pp. 117–119.

1. A widespread response to uncertain situations is the growth of magical beliefs that reduce ambiguity and thus provide a standard for decision-making and action.[18] Many of the self-images of the businessman serve this function. Consider the following common stereotypes: (a) The businessman as a "man of action," the driving, aggresive, impulsive decision-maker personified. He is pictured as irascible, impatient with assistants, and convinced of the rightness of "the decision" as such. (b) The "intuitionist," who, after sitting in contemplation for a moment, comes intuitively to a decision, which is correct because it "clicks." (c) The "man of common sense" or the "practical man." Such self-images provide a rationale for making decisions in an inherently ambiguous situation and protect the businessman against the inroads on his authority by "experts" who control knowledge that the executive, by virtue of his coordinative position, cannot hope to master. Sutton, *et al.*, suggest that one reason for scapegoating of the government by businessmen lies in their attempt to assign meaning to uncertain situations by blaming outside agents for the occurrence of unfortunate events.[19]

2. A number of reactions to strain also appear in connection with the need to make decisions with little regard for human considerations. The most common rationalization is the image of the "hard-headed" businessman who, in a very competitive business, "cannot afford" the luxury of taking human feelings into account without shirking his responsibilities. A number of business practices that have developed in recent times also cushion the "inhumanity" required of the executive role. An example is "kicking upstairs"—removing an incompetent executive from a position of real responsibility to a "higher position" of less responsibility. Others practiced are "by-passing," "passing indirect hints," "freezing out," by which an unwanted executive is put in the position of wishing to resign, rather than be fired.[20]

The top executive, then, as a coordinator at many levels, is a man ensnarled in many strains. As we have just observed, many of his attitudinal and behavioral adaptations can be viewed as attempts to relieve these strains. The man at lower management levels (junior executive, production manager) is also under strains, but of different kinds. His status and authority are between the top executive and the lower echelons. Frequently his relations with both higher and lower levels are ambiguous. In addition, the lower executive struggles continually with specialized staff officials—engineers, sales officials, personnel managers—over matters of company policy. His adaptations to such ambiguity and conflict frequently include excessive preoccupation with the external symbols of status (number of telephones, number of secretaries, size and position of desk), and a tendency to downgrade and scapegoat specialized staff officials on the grounds of their peripheral connection with the "real business" of the company—production.[21]

[18] The classic statement of the relation between uncertainty and magical beliefs is found in Bronislaw Malinowski, *Magic, Science and Religion and Other Essays* (Garden City, N. Y.: Doubleday, 1955).

[19] *Op. cit.*, pp. 332–336, 368–379.

[20] *Ibid.*, pp. 347–354; Editors of Fortune, *The Executive Life* (New York: Doubleday, 1956), pp. 179–194.

[21] Delbert C. Miller and William C. Form, *Industrial Sociology* (New York: Harper, 1951), pp. 196–207.

76

The Professional Role

We shall first consider the professional as an independent practitioner and then the professional as a member of a staff in an organization.

The term "professional" implies that one "professes" or "believes." All professions, in varying degree, involve a commitment to standards of knowledge and excellence, and a commitment to practice in accord with these standards. At the same time the practitioner is "in business," in the sense that he must in some way charge for his services. This tension between the service and commercial aspects of the professional role reflects in the ways in which professionals charge their clients and advertise their services. As A. M. Carr-Saunders and P. A. Wilson observed in their classic work on the professions:

> The fiduciary relationship between professional and client involves certain restrictions on the professional man's methods of charging. It requires that the practitioner shall be financially disinterested in the advice he gives, or, at least, that the possibility of conflict between duty and self-interest be reduced to a minimum. With this object in view attempts have been made to render the financial terms of the contract aboveboard, so that the client may know how much he is paying, what he is paying it for, and whom he is paying it to. . . . It is clear that we have here the expression of an ideal which passes beyond the mere prohibition of specific forms of indirect remuneration such as might result in a conflict between interest and duty [e.g., owning interest in a drug manufacture, or fee-splitting by physicians]. The whole commercial attitude is condemned. . . . Professional men may only compete with one another in reputation for ability, which implies that advertisement, price-cutting, and other methods familiar to the business world are out.[22]

Free-lance professional practitioners normally charge a fee, either a percentage of the sum involved (e.g., one-third of the settlement for lawyers) or a standard office-call fee. Over time these fees remain "remarkably stable." [23] Such are some of the economic adaptations to the tensions between the professional and commercial pressures in professional roles.

When professionals enter bureaucracies, some old problems persist and some new ones arise. The conflict between their independent commitment to professional standards and their necessary involvement in the commercial interests of the bureaucracy gives rise to tensions and conflicts within the organization. In addition, the ambiguous authority relations between the "experts" of the staff and the managers of the line, the differences in educational background between them, and their differing styles of life, aggravate these tensions and conflicts.[24]

A striking illustration of status-conflict arises in the medical pro-

[22] *The Professions* (Oxford: Clarendon Press, 1933), pp. 426–441.

[23] *Ibid*, pp. 451–460.

[24] Robert K. Merton, "Role of the Intellectual in Public Bureaucracy," *Social Theory and Social Structure*, revised and enlarged edition (Glencoe, Ill.: The Free Press, 1957), pp. 207–224; Herbert A. Shepard, "Nine Dilemmas in Industrial Research," *Administrative Science Quarterly* (1956–1957), 1: 295–309; Melville Dalton, "Conflicts between Staff and Line Managerial Officers," *American Sociological Review* (1950), 5: 342–351.

fession of the Soviet Union, which is dominated and administered by central political authorities. According to Mark Field's summary, the Soviet physician is under pressure from his patients (who often wish to escape coercion or sanctions) to grant medical dispensations from responsibility on non-medical grounds. At the same time he is under pressure from the state to keep the citizens in reasonable health and to limit the number of medical dispensations. Thus caught between the demands of his patients and the state, the physician acts as a kind of cushion and brings some stability to the system.[25]

The Foreman

Another "man in the middle" of conflicting expectations and ambiguity is the foreman in the industrial plant. Recent developments in industry have emasculated this once-important figure in two ways: First, centralized management of control has made him less an independent authority over production and more an implementor of ready-made decisions; second, the centralization of the handling of grievances in the unions has relieved him of certain "human relations" functions. The foreman, thus caught in a role that is simultaneously empty and confusing, often flits among identification with management, identification with workers, and identification with other foremen.[26]

Low-skill workers

A recurring theme in the occupations we have examined is *conflicting* role demands that are met by various attempts to resolve the accompanying strains. For low-skill workers a different theme emerges. Strains in this role (especially that of an assembly-line factory worker) focus not on ambiguity so much as outright threats of deprivation —remuneration may be inadequate; the worker often reaches the "end of the career line" in his twenties and may be discriminated against as he grows older; the opportunities to advance from low-level skill jobs to management appear to be diminishing; the worker may be unemployed during depression; and the minimum skills required of him lead to his boredom and alienation.[27] Most studies of reactions to such strains have focused on ideological reorientation of workers—such as defensive rationalizations about failure, redefining "success" in more limited ways, focusing on out-of-plant goals such as consumption, children's opportunities, and so on.[28] The exact relations between the life situation of the worker and his outlook, however, are still only dimly understood.

[25] "Structured Strain in the Role of the Soviet Physician," *American Journal of Sociology* (1952–1953), 58: 493–502.
[26] Robert David Leiter, *The Foreman in Industrial Relations* (New York: Columbia University Press, 1948), pp. 32–41; Donald E. Wray, "Marginal Men of Industry: The Foremen," *American Journal of Sociology* (1948–1949), 54: 298–301.
[27] Ely Chinoy, *Automobile Workers and the American Dream* (Garden City, N. Y.: Doubleday, 1955), pp. 12–109; Robert H. Guest, "Work Careers and Aspirations of Automobile Workers," *American Sociological Review* (1954), 19: 155–163; Robert C. Stone, "Factory Organization and Vertical Mobility," *American Sociological Review* (1953), 18: 28–35.
[28] Chinoy, *op. cit.*, pp. 82–111; Robert C. Stone, "Mobility Factors as they Affect Workers' Attitudes and Conduct toward Incentive Systems," *American Sociological Review* (1952), 17: 58–64.

78

In addition to the analyses of the major role complexes just considered, economic sociology has produced a number of miscellaneous studies of various roles—the nurse, the housemaid, the janitor, the cabdriver, the marine radioman, the professional dance musician, and others.[29] One especially revealing theme emerges in the analysis of modern American occupational roles. Wage deprivation and subsistence problems have slipped into the background as types of strain, except for some of the unskilled and lower white-collar occupations. Other strains, perhaps subordinate heretofore to wage concerns but also emerging as a function of the growing complexity of the division of labor, are beginning to appear as dominant. These strains concern the difficulties that arise from ambiguous and sometimes conflicting demands for role behavior. The role problem in mid-twentieth-century America, it may be suggested, is more the problem of the "man in the middle" than the nineteenth-century problem of the "exploited worker."

While many excellent case studies have shown the relations among characteristics of occupational roles, strains in these roles, and reactions to strain, occupational sociology is still an underdeveloped field. Only in isolated instances are the causal lines among these variables drawn. Furthermore, in our present state of knowledge it is possible only to assert that a *general* class of strains gives rise to a *general* class of reactions to strain. What is required is systematic studies of each set of variables, and a statement of the special conditions under which particular strains will give rise to a particular reaction. Only then will we be able to state the dynamics of role behavior in the form of specific propositions.

Formal Organizations

Economists have traditionally viewed the firm as an organization that is guided by the criterion of profit-maximization—securing the largest difference between revenue and cost. In analyzing the firm's behavior, certain demand conditions for its products and certain supply curves for the firm itself are posited. The firm's supply curve is a statement of the marginal cost for its distinctive product. Marginal cost depends in turn on the supply-demand relations between the firm and the suppliers of its factors of production. These factors presumably weigh most heavily in the firm's calculation of its course of action.

Having assembled these analytic tools, the economist then asks: How will (or should) a firm behave under different kinds of competition? How much should it produce in order to maximize its profits? At what point will it go out of business? What effects do external economies have on the firm? Since it is customary to assume institutional structure, technology, and tastes as given, the firm's behavior turns out to be a resultant

[29] Ronald G. Corwin, "The Professional Employee: A Study of Conflict in Nursing Roles," *American Journal of Sociology* (1960–1961), 66: 604–615; Vilhelm Aubert, "The Housemaid—An Occupational Role in Crisis," *Acta Sociologica* (1955–1956), 1: 149–158; Ray Gold, "Janitor Versus Tenants: A Status-Income Dilemma," *American Journal of Sociology* (1951–1952), 57: 486–493; Fred Davis, "The Cabdriver and his Fare: Facets of a Fleeting Relationship," *American Journal of Sociology* (1959), 65: 158–165; Jane Cassels Record, "The Marine Radioman's Struggle for Status," *American Journal of Sociology* (1956–1957), 62: 353–359; Peter H. Mann, "The Status of the Marine Radioman: A British Contribution," *American Journal of Sociology* (1957–1958), 63: 39–41; Howard S. Becker, "The Professional Dance Musician and His Audience," *American Journal of Sociology* (1951–1952), 57: 136–144.

79

of the interplay of a number of supply and demand relations, translated into statements of cost and revenue.

Since, according to the economist, the firm's decisions depend so much on market conditions, internal analysis of the firm is not often problematical for him. It does not matter whether the manager has difficulty in enforcing his authority (the economists' model of the firm assumes that decisions are translated into action); it does not matter whether communication processes misfire or backfire in the firm (the economists' model of the firm assumes perfect knowledge in the firm); it does not matter whether the executive is effective in *coordinating* his enterprise. In fact, most of the relevant dimensions analyzing the internal dynamics of bureaucracy do not arise in the economists' traditional view of the firm.

Some have criticized the economists' view of the firm and its relation to profit-maximization. Do firms actually operate on such a narrow criterion? Or do other goals figure prominently in their orientations? Much empirical information indicates that trade unions, government, and other forces play a large role in the behavior of the firm. Yet economists have not gone far in *formally* incorporating these forces into the theory of the firm.[30]

Sociological writings on bureaucracy—many of which concern the firm as an economic bureaucracy—has opened these internal dynamics for direct consideration. Discussing bureaucracy, Max Weber emphasized its formal aspects. These include clearly defined and functionally specific roles, each guided by definite rules; organization of these roles into an unambiguous hierarchy of authority and status; authority by rule rather than by person; positions filled by trained and salaried career bureaucrats.[31] Weber pointed out the efficiency of bureaucracy, contrasting it with councils of elders, household staffs, and other forms. Bureaucracy, Weber argued, makes for maximum efficiency because action is rendered calculable and is perpetrated without regard for personal considerations.

Recent research has come to center on features of bureaucracy that may in fact impede efficiency. Specialization of roles itself presumably reaches a point of diminishing economic returns; though such a point has never been established empirically, presumably it appears when overhead costs begin to exceed the contribution of overhead to the value of the product.[32] Robert Merton and others have shown how ritualism, red tape, and ossification of roles may clog bureaucratic channels of action.[33] Alvin Gouldner and Philip Selznick have shown how inadequate individual leadership may lead to conflict and ineffectiveness in organizations.[34] Peter

[30] Many of the above reservations about the traditional theory of the firm are voiced in the excellent essay, "Some Basic Problems in the Theory of the Firm," by Andreas G. Papendreou, in Bernard F. Haley (ed.), *A Survey of Contemporary Economics*, Vol. II (Homewood, Ill.: Irwin, 1952), pp. 183–219.

[31] "Bureaucracy," in Hans Gerth and C. Wright Mills (eds.), *From Max Weber* (New York: Oxford University Press, 1958), pp. 196–216.

[32] For a discussion of some of the economic limits of specialization, cf. Harvey Leibenstein, *Economic Theory and Organizational Analysis* (New York: Harper, 1960), pp. 105–110.

[33] Robert K. Merton, "Bureaucratic Structure and Personality," *op. cit.*, pp. 195–206.

[34] Alvin W. Gouldner, *Patterns of Industrial Bureaucracy* (Glencoe, Ill.: The Free Press, 1954); Philip Selznick, *Leadership in Administration* (Evanston, Ill.: Row, Peterson, 1957).

80

Blau has shown how certain patterns of competition in bureaucracies may reduce outputs.[35] Finally, the adequacy of communication—up and down the line, between staff and line—has been shown to affect the productivity of the firm.

Many variables employed in the analysis of bureaucracy are the general variables of sociology, including economic sociology. These variables include the descriptive characteristics of social structure—role, communication, norms; the important strains—ambiguity (e.g., faulty communication), deprivation (e.g., loss of status or authority), normative conflict; and a number of reactions to strain—the formation of cliques that resist the purposes of the formal organization, restriction of output, internal conflict, and growth of ideologies and rationalizations. Moreover, these responses to strain are frequently viewed as unanticipated consequences that feed back—favorably or unfavorably—to the formal purposes of the bureaucracy.[36]

In the remainder of our discussion of the productive processes in the economy, we shall illustrate the areas into which sociological research on organizations has penetrated in the past several decades.

Formal vs. Informal Organization

The formal organization of a bureaucracy is constituted by the statement of the structure of its positions—explicitly describable, containing definite and known obligations, rights, patterns of interaction. This formal organization can be and frequently is represented as an organization chart, complete with positions, specializations, and hierarchical arrangements. Formal organization is explicit, impersonal, and functionally specific.

Organization charts, however, do not tell the whole story of bureaucratic interaction. A hive of informal groups penetrate this formal structure and affect it in many important ways. These informal groups are generally small (e.g., friendship cliques), personal, and based on implicit understandings and loyalties.

What are the relations between formal and informal organization? Or, as the question is sometimes put, what are the effects of each on one another? First, formal organization is a major determinant of membership in informal groups. Cliques seldom extend very far across authority lines to include both workers and managers; to a lesser extent, staff and line also provide criteria for clique membership. As we shall see, however, other conditions affect membership in informal groups. Formal organizations also constitute a backdrop of rules and standards of conduct around which conformity and deviance—and their feedbacks—develop.

According to Barnard's account, the major functions of informal organization are to facilitate communication that may be impeded by formal channels, to maintain cohesiveness in the organization as a whole, and to maintain the sense of personal integrity of the individual in the organization.[37] In performing these functions, informal groups engage in frequent interaction on the job (horseplay, joking, gambling) and off the job (golf,

---

[35] Peter M. Blau, "Co-operation and Competition in a Bureaucracy," *American Journal of Sociology* (1953–1954), 59: 530–535.

[36] James G. March and Herbert A. Simon, with the collaboration of Harold Guetzkow, *Organizations* (New York: Wiley, 1958), pp. 36–47.

[37] *The Functions of the Executive*, p. 122.

bowling, playing cards). Sometimes this interaction—while not immediately related to the work situation as such—operates as a way of exercising social control over members of informal groups; this control often turns out to be an extremely powerful determinant of behavior on the job.

Occupational position in a formal organization is probably the most important single determinant of the membership cliques.[38] In addition, several other factors influence which individuals will become members: ecological and temporal factors (cliques are most often composed of persons who work near one another on the same shift, with the same times for lunch hours and coffee breaks); sexual factors (in general cliques in bureaucracies tend to be one-sex groups); racial and ethnic factors (segregation between Negro and white cliques is especially pronounced).

What are the relations between the attitudes and behavior of informal groups and the productivity of the formal organization? This question strikes directly at the relations between sociological variables (roles, cliques, sanctions) and economic variables (output). Unfortunately the answers to the question are conflicting.

Louis Schneider and Sverre Lysgaard have suggested four possible relations between morale at the informal level and effectiveness at the formal level: (1) high morale and effectiveness; (2) low morale and ineffectiveness; (3) high morale and ineffectiveness; (4) low morale and effectiveness.[39] Because many industrial sociologists have focused on studies of restriction of output,[40] they have tended to stress the first two relations as follows: High worker morale feeds back positively to productivity; low morale results in slowdown and work restrictions and feeds back negatively. Even in these two cases, however, it is necessary to distinguish between morale *vis à vis* management and morale *vis à vis* the informal group itself. In some situations workers may be thoroughly demoralized from the standpoint of management's goals, yet at the same time have very high morale among themselves. In such situations workers might be able to create the fourth type of relation—high morale and ineffectiveness. In still other cases investigators have found examples in which worker morale is low by any index but in which productivity remains high.[41] In still other situations, such as the example from automation cited above, in which the pace of production is outside worker control altogether, worker-morale—whether high or low—might have very little to do with productivity.

The following lesson emerges from the preceding paragraph: Productivity in formal organizations is a phenomenon with many determinants, of which informal work group morale is one; informal work group morale is a phenomenon which contains many dimensions. To hope for any simple causal relations between morale and productivity is illusory.

[38] John James, "Clique Organization in a Small Industrial Plant," *Research Studies of the State College of Washington* (1951), 19: 125–130.

[39] " 'Deficiency' and 'Conflict' in Industrial Sociology," *op. cit.*, p. 56.

[40] F. J. Roethlisberger and William J. Dickson, *Management and the Worker* (Cambridge: Harvard University Press, 1947); Stanley B. Matthewson, *Restriction of Output among Unorganized Workers* (New York: Viking, 1931); Conrad M. Arensberg and Geoffrey Tootell, "Plant Sociology: Real Discoveries and New Problems," in Mirra Komarovsky (ed.), *Common Frontiers of the Social Sciences* (Glencoe, Ill.: The Free Press and the Falcon's Wing Press, 1957), pp. 315–319.

[41] William J. Goode and Irving Fowler, "Incentive Factors in a Low Morale Plant," *American Sociological Review* (1949), 14: 618–624.

The task at hand in industrial sociology is to isolate the conditions under which morale has an adverse effect on productivity, the conditions under which it has a positive effect, and the conditions under which it has no effect. This means that the operative variables are not nearly so gross as the complex we refer to as "informal organization," which actually conceals a hive of variables within itself.

Authority

As we have seen, many students of informal group relations are preoccupied with two variables: morale and output. The same variables dominate the concern with authority in industrial sociology. Specifically, the issue boils down to the relations between type of supervision (typically described in terms of an authoritarian-democratic dimension) and worker morale. Many studies reveal that worker morale is higher under "employee-centered" leadership than under leadership oriented to technical standards of efficiency. An accompanying finding is that high-morale workers cooperate better with one another and with management and thus affect productivity positively.[42] Most of the experiments and field studies on supervision have been carried out in countries with democratic traditions—especially the United States and Great Britain. Societies with more authoritarian traditions might not display the same results.

Closely related to the relations between supervision and morale are the relations between the character of employee participation in decisions to innovate and the willingness of employees to accept innovations. In a survey of the published material, Michael Stewart found two competing "schools" on this issue. The first maintains that industrial changes themselves are not so threatening to the worker as the way they are introduced; correspondingly, this school argues for active worker participation. The second school maintains that while participation may make a difference in some cases, employee "resistance stems from very real anxieties about employment, status, job-content, etc." [43] This division of opinion is reminiscent of the divergent points of view between the Conflict of Interest and the Human Relations approach outlined above.[44]

Excellent studies of Soviet industry by Berliner and Granick show the importance of the authority and informal group relations in comparative context.[45] Soviet managers, these studies reveal, find themselves under strain—pressured from above by political directives, production targets, and the promise of premiums if they meet these targets; but at the same time beleaguered by bottlenecks in the distribution of raw materials and other supplies. Stated very simply, the managers are asked to meet production targets but do not have ready access to the necessary facilities.

One common reaction to these strains is the appearance of semi-institutionalized forms of deviance by Soviet managers. Examples of de-

---

[42] Viteles summarized the numerous experiments and field studies in *op. cit.*, pp. 161–162.

[43] "Resistance to Technological Change in Industry," *Human Organization* (Fall 1957), 16: 36–37.

[44] P. 43.

[45] Joseph S. Berliner, *Factory and Manager in the USSR* (Cambridge: Harvard University Press, 1957); David Granick, *Management of the Industrial Firm in the USSR* (New York: Columbia University Press, 1954).

viance are saving a "slack" of production goods as a sort of backlog that may be used in meeting future targets; misrepresenting accounts and books; engaging in sub-quality production to reach the target level of output. Apparently the Soviet political authorities tread a thin line between tolerating this deviance and cracking down on it when it threatens to get out of hand.

From the sociological standpoint, one of the most interesting adaptations to the Soviet manager's dilemma is the growth of a phenomenon known as *blat*, or the "use of personal influence in obtaining certain favors to which the firm or individual is not legally or formally entitled." [46] The manager who engages in this practice uses an effective middleman (the *tolkach*), usually a person with whom he has some personal tie (kinship or friendship, for example). By relying on this personal tie—combined at times with monetary recompense for the *tolkach*—the manager can often secure otherwise unobtainable supplies.

Status

Two dimensions we have stressed in the analysis of bureaucracy are division of labor (occupational roles) and authority. Both are important determinants of a person's general status in a bureaucracy. In general, the person who wields authority (a manager, for instance) has a higher status than a person lower down the line; a person with a white-collar job in the organization is likely to have a higher status than a manual worker. In addition, the level of remuneration (which is correlated with, but not identical to, occupation and authority) determines an individual's over-all status in an organization. Several other determinants of status are "imported" from outside the workplace: age (older persons, up to a limit, occupy higher positions); sex (males occupy higher positions); and racial or ethnic background (Negroes, especially, are relegated to lower positions).

Since so many criteria determine an individual's status in an organization, it is evident that a major focus of strain is ambiguity about one's actual status. One is never completely certain which of the criteria—authority, prestige, remuneration, seniority—are most important, or exactly where one stands on each criterion. One consequence of this ambiguity is the tendency for persons to become fixated on objective identifiable *symbols* of status (such as number of secretaries per office, amount of floor space per office). Many conflicts in organizations revolve about the distribution of symbols rather than the distribution of the determinants of status underlying these symbols.[47]

A common characteristic of status systems in formal organizations is a certain "tension toward crystallization" of several determinants of status, such as income, prestige, age, sex, and authority. This tension rests on the assumption that people are comfortable if they and their co-workers are *either* high or low on *all* features of status, uncomfortable if they are high on some and low on others. In a study of clerical workers, for instance, George Homans concluded that filing clerks—whose jobs were repetitive, tiring, low paid, and closely supervised (in short, low on all aspects of

[46] Berliner, *op. cit.*, pp. 182.

[47] For a brief discussion of the importance of symbols, cf. Barnard, "Functions and Pathologies of Status Systems in Formal Organizations," in *Organization and Management*, pp. 207–244.

status)—had few status problems. "While the filing clerks did not like their job," Homans observes, "they felt, in effect, it was just and right they should have it." The ledger clerks, on the other hand, whose job was better on some but not all counts than other positions, showed considerable dissatisfaction and continued efforts to "bring all the status factors in line in their favor." [48] This tendency for all aspects of status to be brought into line with one another underlies many conflicts in industrial settings—disputes over bringing wage and skill differentials into line, opposition to promoting a young executive too rapidly for his age and experience, opposition to women in positions of authority, and opposition to elevating Negroes into high-level jobs.

Communication

A fundamental condition for effective operation in a bureaucracy is a free flow of information and orders. If information is misunderstood, lacking altogether, distorted in passage, or too slow in arriving, confusion, uncontrolled suspicions, and normative conflict arise. Many studies of industrial bureaucracy have uncovered typical points of bottleneck and distortion in the passage of information. Up and down the line the problems are distortion and omission at each level; subordinates "cover up" information they do not wish to have known by their superiors, and foremen "soften" orders out of sympathy with workmen. Particularly disturbing to most bureaucracies is the practice of "jumping the line"— i.e., sending information and grievances from low levels in the hierarchy of authority directly to high levels, thus subverting the ability of the middle levels to control or censor this information.

Structural Changes

Many of the problems of economic bureaucracies discussed so far may arise *within* a given structure of the division of labor. The occurrence of structural changes—sometimes very small ones—may lead to even more complicated reactions and adjustments. The most familiar example of structural change is the introduction of new technology —and the accompanying disruption of work routines, obsolescence of skills, unemployment and loss of status.[49] Less severe structural changes are the introduction of unannounced changes in rules and regulations and the introduction of a new form of payment (e.g., piece-rates, commissions).[50]

In the past decade an interest in the effects of succession (or turnover in personnel) on the industrial bureaucracy has been stimulated in part by Alvin Gouldner's excellent study of succession in a gypsum plant.[51] Gouldner traced the way in which the arrival of a new manager (with new, strict company policies) shook up established patterns of interaction,

---

[48] "Status Among Clerical Workers," *Human Organization* (Spring 1953), 12: 9–10.

[49] For a particularly dramatic example of the effects of technological innovation on a whole community, cf. W. F. Cottrell, "Death by Dieselization: A Case Study in the Reaction to Technological Change," *American Sociological Review* (1951), 16: 358–365.

[50] George Strauss, "The Set-up Man: A Case Study of Organizational Change," *Human Organization* (Summer 1954), 13: 17–25. Nicholas Babchuk and William J. Goode, "Work Incentives in a Self-determined Group," *American Sociological Review* (1951), 16: 679–687.

[51] *Op. cit.*, pp. 70–101.

created a hiatus in the chain of command, led older officials of the company to oppose him and mobilize rank-and-file sentiment against him, and so on. More recently Robert Guest has studied the effects of the arrival of a new manager whose emphasis was not on discipline and rule-enforcement, but rather on worker participation in decisions. Correspondingly, according to Guest's study, his arrival did not stir the conflict and loss of morale observed in Gouldner's study. Indeed, in Guest's study the arrival of a new manager increased the effectiveness of authority.[52]

Distribution and Exchange

The Comparative Analysis of Exchange Systems

Our exposure to economic thought for two centuries has led us often to assume that the exchange of economic goods and services occurs in a market. Even in our own market-dominated society, however, we must contend with several forms of exchange that defy analysis by traditional economic categories of supply and demand, price, interest, profit, rent, and rational calculation of economic gain:

1. The gift for a bride or baby, the services of a friend's wife who prepares dinner, the "good turn"—all are exchanges of goods and services of potential market value. To offer to pay in such exchanges, however, is both inappropriate and insulting. Furthermore, any calculation that enters these exchanges is better attributed to the "rationality" of social reciprocation or status-seeking than to the calculation of economic gain.

2. The redistribution of wealth through charity or progressive taxation is again an exchange of potentially marketable commodities. While the economist may analyze the repercussions of these exchanges in the market, his categories of maximization, prices, and returns seem distant from the social rationale which initiates such redistribution.

3. The mobilization of economic resources for public goals—through eminent domain, taxation, direct appropriation, and selective service—involves the transfer of economic goods and services without the intrusion of an economic market. These exchanges affect the level of production, prices, and income in the market, but the concepts of the market do not explain the original exchange.

On the other hand, we still observe the market in varying degrees of perfection,[53] and we know the value of the economists' theoretical apparatus for explaining and perhaps predicting the course of market behavior. What, then, is the scope of economic analysis in the matter of exchange? What are the spheres of economic calculation that justify the postulate of economic rationality? No matter what our final answers, we must conclude in advance that contemporary economic theory cannot generate specific solutions for *all* the flows of goods and services, even in societies amenable to economic analysis.

In societies where the self-regulating price market is inconspicuous or absent, the categories of economic analysis grow paler. What can we say

[52] *Organizational Change: The Effect of Successful Leadership* (Homewood, Ill.: Dorsey, 1962). For a comparison of the studies by Gouldner and Guest, cf. Guest, "Managerial Succession in Complex Organizations," *American Journal of Sociology* (1962), 68: 47–54, with comment by Gouldner and rejoinder by Guest, pp. 54–56.
[53] Above, pp. 9–10.

sociological analysis of economic processes

about fluctuations of production and prices in the Soviet Union? Certainly the solutions for free-market economies have their limitations. Even more, what can we say about the traditionalized and reciprocal gift-giving among island peoples which does not hint at economic calculation, prices, or gain? What can we say about the post-harvest distribution in Indian villages in which the guiding principle is caste organization? What can traditional international trade theory say about the isolated trading port with fixed exchange equivalencies that rule out price-determination by supply and demand?

Economic anthropologists have been providing ethnographic descriptions of non-market exchange systems for some time.[54] In the past few years a new interest in comparative exchange has been stirred by the appearance of a volume edited by Karl Polanyi, Conrad Arensberg, and Harry Pearson.[55] Roaming through the records of Babylon, Mesopotamia, Greece, Mexico, Yucatan, the Guinea Coast, and village India, they sketch a picture of the separation of trading practices from the familiar practices of free-market exchange. In addition, the authors prepare a critique of the analytic power of traditional economic theory and suggest some alternative categories for a better comparative economics.

On the basis of their studies, Polanyi and his associates suggest that economic activities fall into three main patterns of exchange. The first, which they call *reciprocative*, is illustrated by the ritualized gift-giving among families, clans, and tribes—as analyzed, for instance, by Malinowski and Mauss.[56] Another illustration is found among farmers of many civilizations, who frequently "pitch in" to work for one another, especially at harvest times. Economic calculation, price payments, and wages are typically absent in these types of exchanges. Goods or services are given because it is traditional to do so; the only principle of calculation is the loose principle that the giving and receiving of goods or services should "balance out" among the exchanging parties in the long run.

The second pattern of exchange is *redistributive*. This involves bringing economic goods and services to a central source—usually governmental—and then redistributing them throughout the populace. Polanyi, Arensberg, and Pearson identify several instances of this exchange pattern in ancient Asian and African civilizations. Modern examples are organized charity and progressive taxation. Like reciprocative exchange, redistributive patterns are characterized by an absence of economic calculation and price payments. In this case the principle of calculation seems to be one of "justice"—i.e., what each class of recipients traditionally deserves.[57]

The third pattern of exchange, more familiar in modern Western civilization, is termed, simply, *exchange*. In this case economic goods and services are brought into a market context. Prices are not standardized on the basis of tradition, but result from bargaining for economic advantage.

Polanyi, Arensberg, and Pearson argue that formal economic analysis is equipped to handle only the third type of exchange, and that a different

[54] Above, pp. 17–18.
[55] *Trade and Market in the Early Empires* (Glencoe, Ill.: The Free Press and the Falcon's Wing Press, 1957).
[56] Above, pp. 18–19.
[57] For a criticism and extension of the notion of redistribution, see my review article, "A Comparative View of Exchange Systems," *Economic Development and Cultural Change* (1959), 7: 173–182.

brand of economic theory is needed to analyze exchange systems that are embedded in non-economic contexts. In fact, redistributive and reciprocative systems might be studied fruitfully by examining kinship, stratification, and political systems rather than economic activities as such. Clearly we must modify the assumptions of traditional economics, which have evolved in the study of market economies alone, if we are to create a more comprehensive comparative economics.

Non-economic Elements in Market Systems

Thus far we have focused on exchange systems that are dominated by sanctions other than economic supply and demand. Even in exchange systems dominated by the price complex, we can observe the intrusion of sociological variables. In the remaining discussion of distribution and exchange, we shall sample the empirical research that illuminates three types of markets: the market for labor services, the market for entrepreneurial services, and the market for consumers' goods.

The Labor Market

A central theme in the imperfection of the labor market is the accent on security. This theme underlies workers' concerns with controlling the supply of jobs through closed shop and apprentice control, seniority, layoff rules, severence pay, guaranteed annual wage, and their broader concerns with maintaining full employment through public policy, compensating for unemployment, and so on. Unlike markets for entrepreneurial services (which is built on risk), capital funds, and consumers' goods, then, the labor market is dominated by a concern with security.[58]

Why should this be so? Labor supply emanates above all from the household or family unit.[59] The family, moreover, has as its central functions—in modern society almost as its only functions—the socialization of the young and the expression of emotions and tensions of the family members. The loss of income or employment seriously threatens the performance of these delicate functions. [60] We find in most societies certain institutionalized arrangements—poor laws, minimum-wage laws, insurance, charity, compensation, welfare funds—that insure a family against "bankruptcy" in the usual business sense. A family may break up, but it is felt that it should not do so for reasons of pure and simple insolvency. Thus we frequently find institutional arrangements that guarantee a "floor" of economic security for families and an element of stability of its income and employment. Such arrangements stem from the distinctive sociological functions of the family.

Why should not the market for consumers' goods—which involves the household as well—be characterized by a similar preoccupation with security? The answer lies in the nature of occupational roles. The bread-

---

[58] Lloyd G. Reynolds, *Labor Economics and Labor Relations*, 3rd ed. (Englewood Cliffs, N. J.: Prentice-Hall, 1960), pp. 10–12. This is not to say that the concern with security "explains" everything that unions ask for and do. See above, pp. 52–53, for a comparison of several schools of thought on the origin of industrial disturbances.

[59] Talcott Parsons and Neil J. Smelser, *Economy and Society* (Glencoe, Ill.: The Free Press, 1956), pp. 53–56.

[60] E. Wight Bakke, *Citizens Without Work* (New Haven: Yale University Press, 1940), pp. 109–242.

sociological analysis of economic processes

winner typically has an all-or-none relation with his job; he is either employed or unemployed. If unemployed, his *total* flow of income stops.[61] In the market for consumers' goods, the family spreads its expenditures over a wide range of items, none of which dominates the budget in a way comparable to the work role of its breadwinners.[62] All the family's eggs are never in one consumer's basket.

So much for the factors that condition the broad structuring of the labor market. Considerable research has been conducted on detailed aspects of allocation and performance within a labor market—especially on labor mobility (or turnover) and absenteeism.

Several economic and social factors influence the rate of labor turnover. During times of prosperity the rate of voluntary labor mobility from job to job rises; during depression this rate falls. Involuntary layoffs increase during depression and decrease during prosperity. Economic fluctuations constitute perhaps the most important single determinant of labor mobility. Other influences are occupation (the average turnover of teachers, for instance, is much lower than that of factory workers); age (older workers tend to change jobs less); sex (women move in and out of the labor force more than men, but probably do not move geographically and occupationally so much); and race (Negro men tend to show higher mobility rates than white men). Labor unions *directly* reduce rates of quitting by their pressure for seniority, their opposition to newcomers to plants, and their grievance procedures that help solve labor problems short of forcing the laborer to quit work. Insofar as unions agitate for full-employment programs (and prosperity), however, they *indirectly* increase voluntary rates of quitting and decrease involuntary layoffs.[63]

Research conducted under the auspices of the Tavistock Institute in London focuses on the internal conditions of the "factory as an industrial institution," as a source of determinants of labor turnover. Particular determinants that are stressed are the factory's authority patterns, internal conflicts among departments and within departments, and so on—all of which presumably augment quit rates. Several items of research appear to strengthen their arguments, but others challenge their conclusions.[64]

Some of the conditions that appear to encourage absenteeism are high wages (which lead to the backward-sloping supply curve and a preference for leisure); distance of residence from a plant; size of firm (which is undoubtedly related to morale); occurrence of holidays (absenteeism drops just before holidays); age (young men display absenteeism more than old); marital status (single more than married men); and arduousness of work

[61] These statements must be qualified by the facts that some families have more than one breadwinner and that, especially in modern times, some unemployment compensation often awaits the unemployed.

[62] In expenditures on health and education, however, both of which are intimately tied to the family's own functions, the same concern with security appears.

[63] Reynolds, *op. cit.*, pp. 311–312, 390–392; Herbert S. Parnes, *Research on Labor Mobility* (New York: Social Science Research Council, 1954), pp. 140–143; Hilde Behrend, "Normative Factors in the Supply of Labour," *The Manchester School of Economic and Social Studies* (1955), 23: 62–76.

[64] A. K. Rice and E. L. Trist, "Institutional and Sub-institutional Determinants of Change in Labour Turnover," *Human Relations* (1952), 5: 347; Hilde Behrend, "A Note on Labour Turnover and the Individual Factory," *Journal of Industrial Economics* (November 1953), 2: 58–64.

(which encourages absenteeism).[65] In a study of comparative rates of absenteeism in two casting shops, John Fox and Jerome Scott concluded that intelligent management policies can reduce absenteeism and thus minimize the effect of outside factors such as transportation difficulties.[66]

One final feature of the labor market situation deserves mention, even though it does not involve a direct articulation of economic and non-economic variables. This feature concerns the internal political structure of labor unions. Much research on this aspect of labor unions takes as its starting point—implicitly, at least—the thesis of Robert Michels that oligarchic tendencies universally develop in formal organizations, even in those dominated by democratic ideologies.[67] In labor unions these tendencies are presumably evidenced by poor attendance at meetings, by increasing lengths of tenure among union officers, and by the centralization of the unions' decision-making process.[68] Under some circumstances these tendencies may be counteracted within a union.[69] Moreover, some research suggests that the upward flow of political influence has not necessarily diminished in labor unions, but rather has changed its form. Even though attendance at union meetings falls off (thus giving the impression of mass apathy), informal primary-group interaction at the shop level indicates that those who attend meetings "represent" the opinions of many workers who have talked through the issues in informal conversation beforehand.[70] Perhaps, then, the primary group should be "discovered" in the union, as it has been in the industrial plant by the industrial sociologists.

The Market for Entrepreneurial Services

In one sense the market for entrepreneurs is a market for labor. But the contribution of this kind of labor is sufficiently distinctive to deserve special consideration. Unlike many laborers, the entrepreneur undertakes a risk in reorganizing the factors of production. The form of entrepreneurship varies widely; the function may be performed by an individual businessman, in the engineering department of a firm, in a civil service agency, to name a few. Whatever its social form, however, the place of entrepreneurship in economic development is critical.

[65] George B. Baldwin, *Beyond Nationalization: The Labor Problems of British Coal* (Cambridge: Harvard University Press, 1955), pp. 208–225; John B. Knox, "Absenteeism and Turnover in an Argentine Factory," *American Sociological Review* (1961), 26: 424–428; F. D. K. Liddell, "Attendance in the Coal-Mining Industry," *British Journal of Sociology* (1954), 5: 78–86.

[66] "Absenteeism: Management's Problem," *Business Research Studies* No. 29 (December 1943), Vol. 30, No. 4.

[67] Robert Michels, *Political Parties* (New York: Dover, 1959).

[68] Joseph Goldstein, *The Government of British Trade Unions* (London: Allen & Unwin, 1952), especially pp. 269–271; Eli Ginsberg, "American Labor Leaders: Time in Office," *Industrial and Labor Relations Review* (1947–1948), 1: 283–293; George Strauss and Leonard R. Sayles, "Occupation and the Selection of Local Union Officers," *American Journal of Sociology* (1952–1953), 58: 585–591; Strauss and Sayles, "The Local Union Meeting," *Industrial and Labor Relations Review* (1952–1953), 6: 206–219.

[69] Seymour Martin Lipset, Martin A. Trow, and James S. Coleman, *Union Democracy* (Glencoe, Ill.: The Free Press, 1956).

[70] Joseph Kovner and Herbert J. Lahne, "Shop Society and the Union," *Industrial and Labor Relations Review* (1953–1954), 7: 3–14.

The essence of entrepreneurial activity is the disruption of existing patterns of production and the initiation of new patterns.[71] In the genesis of entrepreneurship the Weber thesis becomes relevant once again. The attitudes favorable to systematic exploitation of the social and cultural world that emerged from the ascetic Protestantism encouraged, among other things, entrepreneurial activity. This complex of Protestantism combined with certain distinctively American values to give this country an extremely fruitful breeding group for individualistic entrepreneurial activity and economic growth.[72] Competitive nationalistic values may also encourage entrepreneurship, but in this case entrepreneurial innovation more often takes a political form. Van der Kroef, basing his views on the Indonesian experience, has argued that nationalism has hindered entrepreneurial activity in that country. Anti-Dutch and anti-Chinese feeling has given rise to an image of the entrepreneur as a sinister, untrustworthy figure; furthermore, Van der Kroef asserts, Indonesians have come to expect not dynamic economic growth from their government but rather security and a place in the state bureaucracy.[73]

Cultural values such as Protestantism or nationalism, however, do not by themselves produce entrepreneurs. Individuals have to be motivated to undertake entrepreneurial activity in the name of these values. How is this accomplished? Some have argued that early socialization of the child is critical in motivating individuals to become constructive deviants in the economic realm.[74] Early socialization does not, of course, necessarily run counter to the influence of cultural values; it may complement them.

In addition to cultural and personality determinants, social structural factors are important in determining whether motivated entrepreneurs succeed. Some have pointed to the importance of blocked alternative paths to prestige; nonconformists in England, for instance, were relatively unable to work their way into the clerical, military, and political elites in pre-industrial Great Britain. Economic activity thus was indirectly encouraged as a means to societal rewards.[75] More broadly, the institutionalization of achievement and universalism in the social structure provides a setting in which entrepreneurs can move resources by economic sanctions.

Finally, entrepreneurship depends on such economic determinants

---

[71] An expanded definition is given by Arthur H. Cole, "Entrepreneurship and Entrepreneurial History: The Institutional Setting," in Harvard University Research Center in Entrepreneurial History, *Change and the Entrepreneur: Postulates and Patterns for Entrepreneurial History* (Cambridge: Harvard University Press, 1949), p. 88. Bert F. Hoselitz has drawn the contrast between industrial entrepreneurship—which does indeed disrupt existing production patterns—and commercial entrepreneurship, which is the ability to capitalize on market transactions—and which does not reallocate factors of production. "Entrepreneurship and Economic Growth," *American Journal of Economics and Sociology* (1952–1953), 12: 97–110.

[72] Thomas C. Cochran, "Role and Sanction in American Entrepreneurial History," in Harvard University Research Center in Entrepreneurial History, *op. cit.*, pp. 171–173.

[73] Justus M. Van der Kroef, "The Indonesian Entrepreneur: Images, Potentialities and Problems," *American Journal of Economics and Sociology* (1959–1960), 19: 413–425.

[74] David McClelland, *The Achieving Society* (Princeton: Van Nostrand, 1961); Everett E. Hagen, *On the Theory of Social Change* (Homewood, Ill.: Dorsey, 1962), Chaps. 5–8.

[75] Yale Brozen, "Determinants of Entrepreneurial Ability," *Social Research* (1954), 21: 344–349; Hagen, *op. cit.*, pp. 240 ff.

as availability of profits (or corresponding political and prestige rewards), access to capital funds, and an appropriate market for new products.[76]

These several determinants of entrepreneurial activity have not been combined in such a way as to allow for specific predictions of the appearance of clusters of entrepreneurial ability. Rather, the determinants constitute a list of contributing factors, for each of which certain historical instances of association with entrepreneurship can be enumerated. But this is not sufficient. As David Landes has argued, entrepreneurial daring is "to be found in greater or less degree all over the world." [77] The research group on entrepreneurship at Harvard was able to locate sometimes vigorous entepreneurial activity among many kinds of agents—among the nobility of many lands (traditionally assumed to be without initiative in economic activity), and even among Russian serfs (often thought to display the essence of economic conservatism).[78] What is required in the analysis of entrepreneurship is not only a longer list of determinants, but also their combination into distinctive *patterns*; only in this way can explanations of the differential occurrence of entrepreneurship be made more precise.

Market for Consumers' Goods

We shall mention only two aspects of the market for consumers' goods—the one-price system and the role of advertising.

Bargaining through haggling and preferential pricing based on particularistic ties (e.g., charging less to members of one's ethnic group) have diminished—though not disappeared—in contemporary Western market structures. In their place has arisen the practice of standard pricing for a product; the purchaser may accept or reject the price, but is not normally able to modify it. Two structural features that underlie this one-price system are the depersonalization of the market and the complexity of the market. With the rise of centralized production and mass distribution, the personal ties between sellers and buyers have weakened. Accordingly, new standards of trustworthiness (other than particularistic ties) have been introduced into the market—standard pricing for all comers, the use of guarantees on products, the use of standard brand names, and so on. In addition, products have become so complex and diversified that it becomes difficult for the consumer to assess the technical quality of the original product (e.g., a television set) and servicing it may require.[79]

As the market becomes more depersonalized and complex, advertising arises as one of the primary means of influencing customers. In one respect advertising is a functional equivalent for personal contacts between sellers

---

[76] Brozen, "Determinants of Entrepreneurial Ability," *op. cit.*, pp. 352–362. Williams has attributed some of the failure of the Chinese in Indonesia to become entrepreneurs to the lack of Chinese banks and the inhospitality of European banks to the Chinese middlemen. Lea E. Williams, "Chinese Entrepreneurs in Indonesia," *Explorations in Entrepreneurial History* (October 1952), V: 342–344.

[77] David S. Landes, "A Note on Cultural Factors in Entrepreneurship," *Explorations in Entrepreneurial History* (1949), I: 8–9.

[78] See the various articles in Vol. VI, No. 2 of *Explorations in Entrepreneurial History*; also Henry Rosovsky, "The Serf Entrepreneur in Russia," *Explorations in Entrepreneurial History* (May 1954), VI: 207–233.

[79] See Parsons and Smelser, *op. cit.*, pp. 157–159. For a case study of the one-price system in watch-repairing, cf. Fred L. Strodtbeck and Marvin B. Sussman, "Of Time, the City, and the 'One Year Guaranty': The Relations between Watch Owners and Repairers," *American Journal of Sociology* (1955–1956), 61: 602–609.

and buyers. Many studies on the actual influence of advertising on buyers have been conducted, but much of our knowledge rests on received folklore and the assertions of interested parties. In addition, there has developed over the past decades a kind of image of the consumer as "one of a captive audience of docile birds charmed and terrified by serpentine advertisers." [80] This image undoubtedly stems from a sort of fantasy of omnipotence held by the advertising profession and those who fear its effects.

As indicated, little is known about the quantitative impact of advertising on the consumer. One piece of recent research, however, has yielded insights concerning the form this influence might take. In an investigation of community buying, voting, and other activities, Elihu Katz and Paul Lazarsfeld isolated what they call the "two-step" flow of influence. Any given community is composed of certain "influentials," who do in fact maintain close touch with national and international advertising. The remainder of the buyers, normally out of touch with or uninfluenced by advertising, are nonetheless influenced *personally*, largely through informal contact in the community, by the "influentials." [81] This research adds complexity to the model of mass influence by mass media; it also marks the "discovery" of the primary group (in which personal, rather than mass influence is the keynote) in the field of consumption, as it has been discovered in productive contexts by industrial sociologists.

The Process of Consumption

A convenient starting point for the analysis of consumption is utilitarianism, which dominated economic thought in the early nineteenth century. The dominant feature of utilitarian thought is that while it held human wants to be an important determinant in the production and distribution of goods and services, it rested on the assumption that in society these wants were essentially *structureless*—i.e., random in variation in society and to be taken as "given data" for every case of economic analysis.[82] Much of the history of consumption theory in economics during the past century has been marked by an attempt to read some psychological or social structure (especially the former) into the concept of demand.

One significant modification of the classical position came at the hands of Alfred Marshall (1842–1924), who incorporated at least some primitive notions of psychological and social structure into demand theory. Taking the concept of elasticity, which had developed in past decades in English classical economics, and the concept of marginality, which had been developed by the Austrian school as well as other thinkers, Marshall built some psychological structure into wants. By the principle of diminishing marginal utility, Marshall held that the utility of a product diminishes as an individual acquires more of it. The extent to which this effect occurs depends, for Marshall, on the elasticity of the demand for the product.

In addition, Marshall indicated that in fact many of the wants of human beings are socially structured in relation to cultural and social patterns. His connection between wants and activities leads to this insight.

[80] Lincoln H. Clark, "Preface," in Clark (ed.), *Consumer Behavior: The Dynamics of Consumer Reactions* (New York: New York University Press, 1955), p. vii.
[81] *Personal Influence* (Glencoe, Ill.: The Free Press, 1955).
[82] Talcott Parsons, *The Structure of Social Action* (New York: McGraw-Hill, 1937), pp. 60–69.

Marshall recognized the existence of certain necessaries for subsistence and for different occupations. But in addition he noted the importance of "activities," in which he included ambition and the pursuit of higher social goals, as themselves parts of civilization which systematically generated wants. Though Marshall did not carry this reasoning into formal demand theory, he was arguing that something besides residual wants determine demand; wants depend in part on the type of civilization in which the economy is embedded. In this way Marshall introduced an element of social determination into demand, above and beyond the simply psychological utility functions.[83]

In a very different tradition from Marshall, though writing about the same time, Thorstein Veblen (1857–1929) also suggested, in his famous theory of conspicuous consumption, that something besides randomly assorted individual wants determine the nature of demand. The very wealthy, Veblen argued, choose their patterns of expenditure to underline, symbolize, and fortify their class position *vis à vis* the rest of the community. Again, this marks the introduction of a social variable into the concept of demand, though Veblen never formalized this insight.[84]

In the past several decades the Marshallian theory of demand has been displaced by preference theory, or indifference curve analysis, which stems particularly from the work of Vilfredo Pareto and John Hicks. Marshall began with an individual's relation to a single product; the indifference curve analyst asks rather at what rate will the individual be willing to substitute one product *for another?* For two or more products, the analyst plots a series of points at which the individual is "indifferent" (i.e., he has no reigning preference) for the marginal increment of each product (he would just as soon have an increment of either one). This series of points results in an indifference curve, the exact shape of which depends on the substitutability of the products and the marginal utility of each. The advantages that economists attribute to preference theory are that it eliminates the measurement problems that arise with notions of diminishing marginal utility, and that it brings more than one product into demand theory. From the standpoint of economic sociology, however, preference theory is essentially structureless, for changes in demand depend ultimately only on changes in income of the buyer and price of products. Tastes are "given" from the standpoint of economic analysis.

The work of Keynes brought into sharp focus the balance between consumption and savings; for him the balance between savings and investment behavior played a critical role in his equilibrium theory. Keynes' theory rests on what he called a "fundamental psychological law" concerning the marginal propensity to consume, whereby "when [any modern community's] real income is increased [the community] will not increase its consumption by an equal absolute amount, so that a greater *absolute* amount must be saved." [85] While Keynes admitted that factors other than this law may affect savings, he did not give them a formal place in his

[83] Parsons, *op. cit.*, Chap. IV.

[84] *Theory of the Leisure Class* (New York: Modern Library, 1934). For an attempt to formalize the Veblen effect, as well as other peculiarities of consumption, cf. Harvey Leibenstein, "Bandwagon, Snob, and Veblen Effects in the Theory of Consumer Demand," *Quarterly Journal of Economics* (1950), 64: 183–207.

[85] *General Theory of Employment, Interest, and Money* (New York: Harcourt, Brace, 1936), p. 97.

94

theory. In the end, then, all we need to know in order to assess the savings ratio is the total income of society and the distribution of this income.

The most serious challenge to the Keynesian postulate is found in James Duesenberry's theory of consumption. Basing his case on general sociological and economic evidence, Duesenberry challenged two of Keynes' assumptions: (1) that every individual's consumption behavior is independent of every other individual, and (2) that people who have recently *fallen* from a higher income level to a given income will spend and save in the same manner as people who have *risen* from a lower income level to the same level. To account for the mutual interdependence of consumers' behavior, Duesenberry developed a utility index incorporating the influence of the expenditure of other individuals. Using this "demonstration effect," he argued, contrary to Keynes, that people will not save proportionately more at higher levels of income, but that at every income level the savings ratio will be approximately the same. To incorporate his second challenge to Keynes, Duesenberry argued that people save more when they arrive at their highest income level ever attained than when they have fallen to that level from an even higher one. The principle is that when income falls previous consumption needs will continue until spending adjusts to the new income level.[86]

Duesenberry attempted to fortify his principles by reference to a wide range of data; in a subsequent study, James Tobin collected a great deal of data in an attempt to test the relative adequacy of Keynes' and Duesenberry's formulations; as might be expected, he found that some data supported the one, some the other formulation.[87] From the standpoint of economic sociology, however, neither theory brings many social structural variables to bear on consumption. Keynes' principle allows for the inference either that social structural elements change at the same rate as income changes, or if they change differently, they cancel out in the aggregate. Duesenberry marks an advance insofar as he introduces the effect of one consumer on the other and the effect of the past on the present. But both these effects are essentially "contentless" as far as structural imperatives themselves are concerned; he introduces only a "conformity" principle and an "inertia" principle.

Duesenberry's analysis introduces very general sociological perspectives into demand theory. The recent work of Milton Friedman on his "permanent income theory of consumer behavior" contains a few sociological variables. Basically Friedman holds that the ratio of consumption to permanent (discounted, expected) income is a function of the interest rate, the ratio of assets to permanent income, and "tastes." Friedman mentions that the sociological variables of age and composition of family affect tastes.[88] In a similar theory, Franco Modigliani, R. E. Brumberg, and Albert Ando hold that consumption is a function of current and expected income and assets. Again the expected income is influenced by such factors as age of retirement, the age distribution of the population,

[86] *Income, Savings, and the Theory of Consumer Behavior* (Cambridge: Harvard University Press, 1949).

[87] "Relative Income, Absolute Income, and Saving," in *Money, Trade and Economic Growth: Essays in Honor of John Henry Williams* (New York: Macmillan, 1951), pp. 135–156.

[88] *A Theory of the Consumption Function* (Princeton: Princeton University Press, 1957).

and so on.[89] The sociological variables these theories incorporate are limited to gross demographic indices.

In the past two decades some analysts have displayed a dissatisfaction with deductive theories of diminishing marginal utility and indifference curve analysis. Ruby Turner Norris, for instance, has argued that consumption theory should not be written in terms of diminishing marginal utility "or any alternative of that theory." Rather, she would divide short-term purchases into several categories according to type of expenditure. Especially important are (1) those expenditures which involve no calculation, such as legal obligations (e.g., rent), forced savings for Christmas clubs, income taxes, insurance health plans, and so on; (2) areas in which careful weighing occurs, as in investment in certain stocks on the exchange; and (3) a "dynamic residual," in which the purchaser makes sporadic experimental purchases.[90] While perhaps psychologically more satisfactory than some of the simpler theories of many economists, this theory marks a retreat toward pure description—imitative, rational, and experimental purchases. It does not produce a *theory* of demand, as do the deductive theories of indifference curve analysis and diminishing marginal utility analysis.

An even more radical rejection of economic theory is found in the work of George Katona.[91] Unlike economic theorists, Katona argues that he will not make any universal assumptions about economic behavior, rationality, and the like, but will study economic behavior as it exists. With this somewhat behavioristic approach (combined with a version of Gestalt psychology), Katona attempts to assess people's *attitudes* about spending and saving, the degree to which people plan, and the degree to which their attitudes and plans actually manifest themselves in *buying patterns*. The major research tool which Katona and his associates employ is the survey research method. In general Katona does not develop any generalized theory of consumption behavior; rather, he works with low-level generalizations that relate attitudes, income level, and so on, seldom systematically introducing any social structural variables that affect consumption.

Throughout this critique of consumption theory we have noted a lack of incorporation of social structural variables. Behind this critique lies, of course, our own preference for this kind of demand theory. What kind of theory would this be? We would conceive that consumers classed according to various sociological dimension (social class, race), are differentially involved in social structures; these structures impinge on their spending patterns both at a gross level (e.g., spending-saving ratios) and at a detailed level (e.g., the kinds of consumer items used to symbolize sex roles). Thus, for any given consumer, we would note sex, marital status, age, and position in class structure, and posit certain *levels* and *kinds* of spending and saving that symbolize his involvements in social structural contexts. Then, by aggregating these attachments to such contexts, a con-

[89] Modigliani and Brumberg, "Utility Analysis and the Consumption Function: An Interpretation of Cross-Sectional Data," in K. K. Kurihara (ed.), *Post Keynesian Economics* (New Brunswick, N. J.: Rutgers University Press, 1954), pp. 388–436; Modigliani and Ando, "The 'Permanent Income' and the 'Life Cycle' Hypotheses of Saving Behavior: Comparison and Test," in Irving Friend and Robert Jones (eds.), *Proceedings of the Conference on Consumption and Saving* (Philadelphia, 1960), pp. 49–174.

[90] *The Theory of Consumer's Demand* (New Haven: Yale University Press, 1941), pp. 98–108.

[91] *Psychological Analysis of Economic Behavior* (New York: McGraw-Hill, 1951), Chap. III.

96

sumption function, or rather a series of consumption functions, could be reproduced for incorporation into various theories of demand.

Unfortunately such a program is in the visionary stage. No comprehensive consumption function based on such structural variables has yet been produced.[92] All we possess is a number of somewhat disparate empirical studies that show differential saving and spending patterns on the part of persons classified according to various sociological categories. Let us at least explore some of the implications of these studies.

For any consumption theory it is important to discard the traditional view of the household as the only significant spender and saver. The government, for instance, as well as voluntary associations, business firms, and the like, contribute much to any demand for products, especially in a complex economy. For saving it is perhaps even more important to take into account the behavior of firms, governments, and various institutional savers such as "insurance companies, savings and commercial banks, savings and loan associations, trust companies, trust funds, investment trusts, pension funds, and endowments." [93] While the savings base for these different forms of savers may rest in part in household decisions, the effective determinants of saving and spending behavior of these agencies often cease to depend on household decisions.

For any consumption theory it is necessary to specify the relevant *aspect* of spending and saving to be studied. Is it the ratio of savings and spending? Is it the ratio among different *kinds* of spending (consumer durables, food, clothing)? Is it the ratio among different *kinds* of saving (insurance, cash, stock purchases)?

With regard to food consumption, for instance, the following kinds of social correlates are of some interest: (1) *Sex and age.* Women consume less than men, children less than adults. (2) *Ecology.* Rural populations consume more than urban populations on the average, but variation and product differentiation is greater in urban areas. (3) *Economic resources.* In general those near the starvation level spend almost all their increments of income on food; above this level "Engel's law" takes effect and with increments of income a smaller proportion is spent on food; then in the upper reaches, when sedentary occupations dominate, the absolute amount spent for food may actually decrease in some cases.[94] (4) *Occupational status of family members.* Generally, as the income of family increases at middle-income levels, the proportion of income spent on food diminishes; but if this increase results from the fact that the wife takes a job, the proportion spent on food may *increase*, because of reliance on more service costs on food (e.g., frozen foods), more meals taken out in restaurants, and so on. Such dimensions should be incorporated into an aggregate consumption function for food.

Similar variables—age, family size, race, home-ownership status, and degree of urbanization—affect aggregate savings and spending patterns. It appears, for instance, that the marginal propensity to consume for wage-

[92] For a tentative theoretical formulation, cf. Parsons and Smelser, *op. cit.*, pp. 221–227.

[93] Woodlief Thomas, "The Institutionalization of Savings: Trends and Implications," in Walter W. Heller, Francis M. Boddy, and Carl E. Nelson (eds.), *Savings in the Modern Economy* (Minneapolis: University of Minnesota Press, 1953), p. 169.

[94] Carle C. Zimmerman, *Consumption and Standards of Living* (Princeton: Van Nostrand, 1936), pp. 75–117.

earners is very high, for farmers very low, and for aggregate nonwage-earner non-farm consumers somewhere in between.[95] Negroes generally save more at all income levels than whites, except for high-income southern Negroes, who appear to save less than southern whites at that income level.[96] Social-class conditions the *form* of leisure chosen—whether an individual goes to a cocktail lounge or a bar, to a library or a zoo, to a play or to the movies, and so on.[97] Life-cycle variables also prove to be an important variable in demand—variables such as when children are born, when the house is purchased (other durables are purchased with a house), and so on.[98]

In the construction of any consumption function—for a particular product, for a particular class of products, for consumption in general, or for the consumption-savings ratio—no *particular* sociological variable is to be regarded as the key determinant. Different combinations of sociological variables enter into different statements of consumption functions. What is required for the development of an adequate sociology of consumption is vigorous pursuit of three lines of intellectual activity: first, a re-analysis of existing budget, cross-sectional, attitudinal, and other data to assess which sociological categories appear to contribute the most important sources of variation in consumer demand; second, the conduct of new studies explicitly oriented to the sociological variables of social class, life-cycle, and so on; and third, the attempt to combine different sociological variables into definite models of consumer behavior. This last operation rests in part on the results of empirical research; it also involves, however, the purely logical operation of refining classifications of social variables and combining them into organized patterns of influence, rather than presenting these variables merely as a long list of possibly influential factors.

Conclusion

What lessons may we draw from this long exploration of the impingement of sociological variables on production, distribution, and consumption? There is little doubt of the *general* strength of these sociological variables. Not only is there a sociology of economic life, but this sociology conditions the behavior of strictly economic variables. Again, however, economic sociology is very long on numbers of variables, but very short on adequate data, classifications of variables, and organization of variables into models. Most sociological studies emphasize some single variable (e.g., informal group membership). Little effort is made to show the theoretical relevance of this variable to the corpus of economic theory or the other sociological variables. In economic sociology, then, we need not only more research; we also need improved classification schemes that reduce redundancy in the existing lists of variables, sharpen the differences among them, and cast them in such a way that they can articulate with economic variables. Only in this way can the field produce more than a mere proliferation of new variables and bits of insight.

[95] Lawrence R. Klein, "Keynesian Theory and Empirical Inquiry: A Note on 'Middle-Range' Formulation," in Komarovsky (ed.), *op. cit.*, pp. 384–385.

[96] Lawrence R. Klein and W. H. Mooney, "Negro-white Savings Differentials and the Consumption Function Problem," *Econometrica* (1953), 21: 433.

[97] Alfred C. Clarke, "The Use of Leisure and its Relation to Levels of Occupational Prestige," *American Sociological Review* (1956), 21: 301–307; R. Clyde Whyte, "Social Class Differences in the Uses of Leisure," *American Journal of Sociology* (1955–1956), 61: 145–150.

[98] Nelson N. Foote, "The Autonomy of the Consumer," and William H. Whyte, Jr., "The Consumer in the New Suburbia," in Lincoln H. Clark (ed.), *op. cit.*, pp. 1–24.

sociological analysis of economic processes

sociological
aspects
of economic
development

five

In both Chapters 3 and 4 our analysis had a "time-less" character. We were interested in the mutual influence among economic and non-economic variables at the broad societal level and at the level of concrete economic processes. But we seldom asked how this mutual influence leads to cumulative social and economic changes over time. In this chapter we shall open this inquiry.*

Several Types of Change

Perhaps the simplest kind of change is that which results from the circulation of various rewards, facilities, and personnel through an existing structure. We might refer to this kind of change simply as *social process*. An economic example is the process of allocating goods, services and money in day-by-day market transactions. Sometimes this process gives rise to regularities in the movement of indices—as in inventory cycles, trade cycles, and redistributions of wealth. Outside the economic sphere, similar processes are observable. "Social mobility," for instance, often refers to the movement of persons through a status hierarchy; it does not necessarily involve any structural change in the hierarchy

---

* A portion of this chapter is a revised version of a chapter "Mechanisms of Change and Adjustment to Change," written for a volume entitled *Industrialization and Society*, edited by Wilbert E. Moore and Bert F. Hoselitz, and published by Mouton, The Hague, in collaboration with UNESCO, in 1963.

itself. A political election often involves a redistribution of political power and a turnover of political personnel, but not necessarily any constitutional or legal changes in the political framework. The key defining characteristic of *process*, then, is that change takes place within an existing structure.

A type of change intermediate between social process and changes in social structure is *segmentation*. This refers to the proliferation of additional structural units that do not differ qualitatively from existing units. An example of segmentation is natural population increase, in which new families—but not necessarily a new family structure—are created. A second example is the addition of new firms to the market when demand increases. In both cases segmentation refers to the multiplication of structurally similar units.

Structural change proper, however, involves the emergence of qualitatively new complexes of roles and organizations. In Berle and Means' analysis of the separation of ownership and control in the modern corporation,[1] for instance, the change involved more than the growth of new firms. It involved the growth of new roles (managers, passive stockholders) and a new *type* of organization (the modern corporation).

Though it is possible to separate social process, segmentation, and structural change analytically, the three are intimately associated empirically. Economic innovations (e.g., the establishment of new industries such as railroads) involve structural changes that are of sufficient magnitude to produce, or at least initiate business cycles. Sometimes the segmentation of family units creates population pressure that is difficult to contain in a social system without far-reaching changes in the structure of production and consumption.

In this chapter we shall concentrate on structural changes, emphasizing those that are associated with economic and social development (sometimes called "growth" or "modernization").

Economists' Views of Development

Marx's view of the evolution from feudalism to capitalism to communism involves a series of metamorphoses at the structural level—in the relations among classes, between the state and the economy, and so on. In the past few decades, economists have tended to move away from the analysis of structural changes of this magnitude, and to concentrate on the movement of quantitative economic indices. Accordingly, many economists begin with a notion of growth that is limited to some index such as growth of output per head of population, or steel production, or size of labor force. Such a notion forms the basic dependent variable.

The basic independent variables that determine rates of growth are found in the factors of production—natural resources, capital for investment, labor, and entrepreneurial talent. Other economic variables immediately involved with the supply of these factors are savings, inflation, balance of payments, foreign aid, size of population, and rate of population change.[2]

---

[1] Above, p. 46.

[2] For a review of modern theories of growth that incorporate such variables, cf. Henry J. Bruton, "Contemporary Theorizing on Economic Growth," in Bert F. Hoselitz (ed.), *Theories of Economic Growth* (Glencoe, Ill.: The Free Press, 1961), pp. 243–262.

Economists sometimes investigate what they call "structural change," but this concept is often limited to the relative rates of growth of different industries. As Henry Bruton summarizes the problem of structural change:

> . . . it seems reasonably clear that no one narrowly defined industry will continue to grow at a constant percentage rate; rather it may be expected to grow strongly in the period immediately after its inception, and then to taper off as it catches up with the rest of the economy. This means that at any given period of time, a few industries are experiencing vigorous and rapid development and are, as it were, pulling the rest of the economy along. However, this rate of growth does not continue indefinitely. It begins to taper off toward the level of the rate of growth of the economy as a whole; eventually it will fall below the rate, and possibly decline in absolute terms.[3]

After an industry has "caught up," Bruton suggests, its future rate of growth depends on one or more of three immediate economic determinants—population, demand, and technology.

Sociological Aspects of Economic Growth

Behind the immediate economic variables lie a host of cultural, social, and psychological determinants. The savings-investment complex, for instance, is conditioned in particular by the kinship and stratification systems. Inflexible gift-giving rituals may "tie up" consumption in traditional forms and thus make for a low level of savings. The style of life of an aristocracy may make for high levels of consumption. This style of life, moreover, may emphasize savings in the form of heirlooms or jewelry which "freeze" savings so that they cannot be invested in economically productive enterprises. Presently we shall illustrate the effects of non-economic variables on the availability and flexibility of the factors of production, which in turn affect the rate of economic growth.

Later in the chapter we shall inquire into changes in the social structure that are concomitant with, and in some cases determined by, economic development. In analyzing these relations between economic growth and social structure, it is possible to isolate the effects of several interrelated technical, economic, and ecological processes frequently accompanying development: (1) In technology, the change *from* simple and traditionalized techniques *toward* the application of scientific knowledge. (2) In agriculture, the evolution *from* subsistence farming *toward* commercial production of agricultural goods. This means specialization in cash crops, purchase of non-agricultural products in the market, and frequently agricultural wage-labor. (3) In industry, the transition *from* the use of human and animal power *toward* industrialization proper, or "men aggregated at power-driven machines, working for monetary return with the products of the manufactuing process entering into a market based on a network of exchange relations."[4] (4) In ecological arrangements, the movement *from* the farm and village *toward* urban centers. These several processes often occur simultaneously. However, certain technological improvements—e.g., the use of improved seeds—can be introduced without automatically pro-

---

[3] *Ibid*, p. 263.
[4] Manning Nash, "Some Notes on Village Industrialization in South and East Asia," *Economic Development and Cultural Change* (1954–1955), III: 271.

ducing organizational changes; agriculture may be commercialized without accompanying industrialization, as in many colonial countries; industrialization may occur in villages; and cities may proliferate in the absence of significant industrialization, as was the case with many medieval trading centers. Furthermore, the specific social consequences of technological advance, commercialized agriculture, the factory, and the city, respectively, are not in any sense reducible to one another.

Nevertheless, these technological, agricultural, industrial, and ecological changes tend to affect the social structure in similar ways. All give rise to the following typical structural changes that ramify throughout society: (1) Structural differentiation, or the establishment of more specialized and more autonomous structural units. We shall illustrate this process in several different spheres—economy, family, religion, and stratification. (2) Integration, or the establishment of new coordinative structures—especially legal, political, and associational—as the old social order is made obsolete by the processes of differentiation. (3) Social disturbances—mass hysteria, outbursts of violence, religious and political movements—which reflect the social tensions created by the processes of differentiation and integration. Later in the chapter we shall specify these structural changes and show their relations to one another.

Sociological Determinants of Growth

Vicious and Beneficent Circles of Growth

For an analysis of how sociological variables impinge on economic growth, we begin with an economic model expounded by Ragnar Nurkse.[5] Underdeveloped areas, he argues, frequently are caught in a trap of low per-capita output—a trap composed of two vicious circles, one on the side of the *supply* of factors of production, and one on the side of *demand* for products.

On the *supply* side, capital is scarce because of the low capacity of people to save. This low capacity to save is a reflection of the low level of real income. The low level of income is a reflection of low productivity in the economy, which in its turn is due largely to the lack of capital. The lack of capital is a result in part of the small capacity to save, and so the circle is complete. These variables form a system of mutual determination, the net effect of which is to keep the values of all the variables small.

On the *demand* side, inducement to invest may be low because of the limited buying power of the people, which is due to their small low real income. This low real income results from low productivity, which in turn reflects the small amount of capital used in production. The low volume of investment, finally, rests on the small inducement to invest. Again the interaction among all the variables operates to keep every variable low in value.

Much of Nurkse's exposition is devoted to examining the ways in which these vicious circles can be broken. If this can be done—i.e., if it is possible to raise the value of one variable, such as the inducement to invest—all the variables will begin to increase and the result will be a beneficent circle of economic growth. Among the possibilities Nurkse sug-

[5] *Problems of Capital Formation in Underdeveloped Areas* (New York: Oxford University Press, 1962), especially Chap. 1.

sociological aspects of economic development

gests for altering the vicious circles are increasing international trade, diminishing (or at least stopping the growth of) population, removing excess labor from the land, forcing savings, and borrowing internationally. He argues, however, that many of these proposed means are likely to prove ineffective unless entreprenurs plunge into the economy and augment the variable of "inducement to invest"; in so doing they introduce basic structural changes in the factors of production.[6]

Sociological Determinants
of Economic Variables

Nurkse's theory emphasizes the interaction among economic variables, such as savings, investment, consumption, productivity, entrepreneurship, and so on. If we move behind the immediate interplay of these variables, we find that the value of each is determined in part by sociological variables such as kinship, social stratification, and politics.

The Savings-Consumption-Investment Complex

Two aspects of savings are important in the initiation of development. The first is the *level* of savings; here the relevant question is the amount of wealth diverted from current consumption needs. The second aspect is the *form* of savings; while the level of savings may be high enough, these may be "frozen" in jewelry or coins and thus unavailable for investment in economic enterprises. Some determinants of savings behavior are economic—for instance, in those cases where income is so low that all of it must be spent on subsistence. In other cases, however, savings and investment behavior is a resultant of sociological variables such as the stratification or kinship systems.

With regard to the stratification system, most rural peasant societies are dominated by status systems centering on the land. In a summary of studies on savings in southern Asia, Richard Lambert and Bert Hoselitz show how this kind of stratification affects investment behavior:

> In all countries of [Southern Asia] land heads the list of approved possessions. . . . Even wealth earned in non-agricultural pursuits must be converted into land holding to be fully legitimized. In part, this overwhelming emphasis on the acquisition of land is understandable since it is the primary agricultural producer's good, but often it is pursued even when alternative investments [to land] are demonstrably more rewarding. . . . One result of this emphasis on land is that with increasing densities and general inflationary trends, the price of land rises rapidly. . . . In 1960 the price of land [was] 8 to 10 times that of 1939 and it [cost] more than can normally be earned on it in 15 to 20 years. . . .
> If accumulation takes place in other items than land, it is in currency or coins, stored in trunks or buried in a corner of the house, in jewelry and precious metals—the lower classes' insurance—and in stores of grain. The latter may be used not only to ensure a supply for consumption but to speculate on fluctuations in prices over the growing season.[7]

Such arrangements tend to divert savings into relatively unproductive economic channels.

[6] *Ibid.*, pp. 154–156.
[7] "Southern Asia and the West," in Lambert and Hoselitz (eds.), *The Role of Savings and Wealth in Southern Asia and the West* (forthcoming), no pagination in manuscript.

Various traditional rituals also divert wealth from investment. Again, in southern Asia,

> The rites of passage of the life cycle and the union of two families through marriage are embroidered with religious ceremonials. . . . Increments in family wealth call for increased expenditures on religious rituals. Wedding ceremonies, burial ceremonies, and feasts for the dead are sharply graduated by cost. . . . In death ceremonials, the priest going to the house where the body lies instead of waiting at the church, an elaborate ceremony at the church, complete with choir, and church bells, the priest going to the cemetery to make offerings for the dead, a choir singing and a band playing at the grave—all of these can increase the cost of a funeral ten to fifteen times. . . . The graduated elaboration of ceremonials can absorb a major portion of surplus income or past savings which might otherwise find economically more productive uses. While one report fixed the expenditure on ceremonials in rural India at 7.2% of the per capita income, a more revealing figure shows that if the funds spent on marriage and death ceremonies in rural India had been spent on productive capital assets they would have increased such investment by more than fifty per cent.[8]

Such rituals—rooted in family, community and religion—often die hard; they are usually disrupted only when sweeping social changes (e.g., colonialization or urbanization) begin to erode the whole peasant way of life.

Labor Commitment

Economic growth calls for more than investment. Investment funds must be used to hire laborers, often in new industrial settings. Laborers must be brought into a new reward system (wage payments), a new form of authority (supervision on factory premises), and a more impersonal market setting. Peasant societies, with their close kinship relations and their attachment to the land, frequently offer resistance to the recruitment of labor into industrial urban settings. Wilbert Moore has observed of the kinship system in non-industrial societies: "[It] perhaps . . . offers the most important single impediment to individual mobility, not only through the competing claims of kinsmen upon the potential industrial recruit but also through the security offered in established patterns of mutual responsibility."[9]

Entrepreneurship

As Nurkse argues, the innovations of entrepreneurs are essential in the initiation of economic growth. But entrepreneurship, like capital and labor, does not just appear automatically. It is the product of a large number of complex social forces. We noted earlier that different religious and nationalistic traditions offer differential encouragement to the appearance of entrepreneurial talent and activity. Furthermore, traditional family systems—through which the values of religion are fre-

[8] Ibid.
[9] Wilbert E. Moore, Industrialization and Labor (Ithaca and New York: Cornell University Press, 1951), p. 24. For numerous examples, cf. pp. 24–34. A number of specific case studies are found in Wilbert E. Moore and Arnold S. Feldman (eds.), Labor Commitment and Social Change in Developing Areas (New York: Social Science Research Council, 1960).

sociological aspects of economic development

quently perpetrated—differ greatly in their encouragement of entrepreneurial talent.

One of the peculiar features of many traditional peasant and tribal societies is that their kinship-community-religious complex of institutions offer serious obstacles to the effective appearance of entrepreneurs. As a matter of historical fact, economic development (however limited and unbalanced) appeared in these societies only as Western colonial entrepreneurs began to disrupt traditional economic practices. In addition, aggressive nationalism—frequently a by-product in part of colonial domination—becomes a vehicle for the destruction of traditional patterns of economic activity and for entrepreneurial innovation.[10]

Structural Changes
Associated with Development

Variability in the Process of Development

Let us now assume that the vicious circle of poverty has been broken—by what exact mechanism it does not matter for now—and that economic growth has begun. What happens to the social structure under such circumstances?

No simple answer to this question is available, because national differences make for a variety of patterns of development. Processes of economic development may differ in the following ways:

1. Variations in the *pre-industrial conditions* of the country. A society's value-system may be congenial or antipathetic to industrial values. The society may be tightly or loosely integrated. Its level of wealth may be low or high. This wealth may be evenly or unevenly distributed. From the standpoint of population, the society may be "young and empty" (e.g., Australia) or "old and crowded" (e.g., India). The society may be politically dependent, recently independent, or altogether autonomous. Such pre-existing conditions shape the impact of the forces of economic development and make for great differences in national experiences with development.

2. Variations in the *impetus* to development. The pressures to develop may stem from the internal implications of a value-system (as in Weber's theory of ascetic Protestantism), from a desire for national security and prestige, from a desire for material prosperity, or from a combination of these. Political coercion may be used to form a labor force. Or these pressures may be economic, as in the case of population pressure on the land, or loss of handicraft markets to cheap imported products. Or economic and political pressures combine, as in the case of a tax on peasants payable only in money. Or the pressures may be social, as in the case of the desire to escape burdensome aspects of the old order. Such differences influence the adjustment to modernization greatly.

3. Variations in the *path* toward modernization. The development sequence may begin with light consumer industries. Or there may be an attempt to introduce heavy, capital-intensive industries first. The government may take an active or passive role in shaping the pattern of invest-

[10] Rupert Emerson, Lennox A. Mills, and Virginia Thompson, *Government and Nationalism in Southeast Asia* (New York: Institute of Pacific Relations, 1942), pp. 9–11; W. W. Rostow, *The Stages of Economic Growth* (Cambridge: Cambridge University Press, 1960), pp. 27–28; Moore, *Industrialization and Labor*, pp. 94–97.

ment. The tempo of industrialization may be fast or slow. All these affect the nature of structural change and the degree of discomfort created by this change.

4. Variations in the *advanced stages* of modernization. Societies may vary in the emergent distribution of industries in their developed economies. They may vary in the emergent relations between state and economy, state and religion, and so on. While all advanced industrialized societies have their "industrialization" in common, unique national differences remain. For instance, social class differs in its social significance in the United States and Great Britain, even though both are highly developed countries.

5. Variations in the *content and timing of dramatic events* during development. Wars, revolutions, rapid migrations, and natural catastrophes may influence the course of economic and social development.

Because of these sources of variation, it is virtually impossible to discover hard and fast empirical generalizations concerning the evolution of social structures during economic and social development. Our purpose, therefore, in this chapter, is not to search for such generalizations, but to outline certain very general, ideal-type structural changes associated with development. These changes are three: structural differentiation, integration, and social disturbances. On the basis of these changes we may classify, describe and analyze varying national experiences. Variations such as those just described determine in part the distinctive national response to these universal aspects of development, but this in no way detracts from their "universality."

Structural Differentiation
in Periods of Development

The concept of structural differentiation can be employed to encompass many of the structural changes that accompany the movement from pre-industrial to industrial society. Simply defined, differentiation refers to the evolution from a multi-functional role structure to several more specialized structures. The following are typical examples: (1) In the transition from domestic to factory industry, the division of labor increases, and the economic activities previously lodged in the family move to the factory. (2) With the rise of a formal educational system, the training functions previously performed in large part by the family and church are established in a more specialized unit, the school. (3) The modern political party has a more complex structure than tribal factions, and is less likely to be fettered with kinship loyalties, competition for religious leadership, etc. Formally defined, then, structural differentiation is a process whereby "*one* social role or organization . . . differentiates into *two or more* roles or organizations which function more effectively in the new historical circumstances. The new social units are structurally distinct from each other, but taken together are functionally equivalent to the original unit." [11]

Differentiation concerns only changes in role-structure. We should not confuse the concept with two closely related notions. The first of these is the cause or motivation for entering the differentiated role. Wage-labor, for instance, may result from a desire for economic improvement, from

[11] Neil J. Smelser, *Social Change in the Industrial Revolution* (Chicago: University of Chicago Press, 1959), p. 2.

sociological aspects of economic development

political coercion, or even from a desire to fulfill traditional obligations (e.g., to use wages to supply a dowry). These "reasons" should be kept conceptually distinct from differentiation itself. The second notion concerns the integration of differentiated roles. As differentiated wage-labor begins to appear, for instance, there also appear legal norms, labor exchanges, trade unions, and so on, which regulate—with varying degress of success—the relations between labor and management. Such readjustments, even though they sometimes produce a new social unit, should be considered separately from role-specialization in other functions.

Let us now inquire into the process of differentiation in several different social realms.

Differentiation of Economic Activities

Typically in underdeveloped countries production is located in kinship units. Subsistence farming predominates; other industry is supplementary but still attached to family and village. In some cases occupational position is determined largely by an extended group such as the caste. Similarly, exchange and consumption are embedded deeply in family and village. In subsistence agriculture there is a limited amount of independent exchange outside the family; this means that production and consumption occur in the same social context. Exchange systems proper are lodged in kinship and community (e.g., reciprocal exchange) in stratification systems (e.g., redistribution according to caste membership) and in political systems (e.g., taxes, tributes, payments in kind, forced labor). Under such conditions market systems are underdeveloped, and the independent power of money to command the movement of goods and services is minimal.

As the economy develops, several kinds of economic activity are removed from this family-community complex. In agriculture, the introduction of money-crops marks a differentiation between the social contexts of production and consumption. Agricultural wage-labor sometimes undermines the family production unit. In industry it is possible to identify several levels of differentiation. Household industry, the simplest form, parallels subsistence agriculture in that it supplies "the worker's own needs, unconnected with trade." "Handicraft production" splits production and consumption, though frequently consumption takes place in the local community. "Cottage industry," on the other hand, frequently involves a differentiation between consumption and community, since production is "for the market, for an unknown consumer, sold to a wholesaler who accumulates a stock." [12] Finally, manufacturing and factory systems segregate the worker from his capital and frequently from his family.

Similar differentiations appear simultaneously in the exchange system. Goods and services, previously exchanged on a non-economic basis, are pulled more and more into the market. Money now commands the movement of more and more goods and services, and thus begins to supplant—and sometimes undermine—the religious, political, familial or caste sanctions which previously had governed economic activity.

Empirically we may classify underdeveloped or semi-developed economies according to how far they have moved along this line of differen-

---

[12] These "levels," which represent points on the continuum from structural fusion to structural differentiation, are taken from J. H. Boeke, *The Structure of the Netherlands Indian Economy* (New York: Institute of Pacific Relations, 1942), p. 90.

107

tiation. Migratory labor, for instance, may be a kind of compromise between full membership in a wage-labor force and attachment to an old community life; cottage industry introduces extended markets but retains the family-production fusion; the hiring of families in factories maintains a version of family production; the expenditure of wages on traditional items such as dowries also shows this half-way entry into the more differentiated industrial-urban structure. The reasons for these partial cases of differentiation include resistances on the part of the populace to give up traditional ways of life, the economics of demand for handmade products, and systems of racial discrimination against native labor. In any case, the concept of structural differentiation provides a yardstick to indicate the distance which the economic structure has evolved.

Differentiation of Family Activities

One implication of the removal of economic activities from the kinship nexus is that the family loses some of its previous functions, becoming a more specialized agency. The family ceases to be an economic unit of production; one or more members now leave the household to seek employment in the labor market. The family's activities become more concentrated on emotional gratification and socialization. While many compromise arrangements such as family hiring and migratory systems persist, the tendency is toward the segregation of family functions and economic functions.

Several related processes accompany this differentiation of the family from its other involvements: (a) Apprenticeship within the family declines. (b) Pressures develop against the intervention of family favoritism in the recruitment of labor and management. These pressures often lie in the demands of economic rationality. The intervention often persists, however, especially at the managerial levels, and in some cases (e.g., Japan) family ties continue as a major basis for labor recruitment. (c) The direct control of elders and collateral kinsmen over the nuclear family weakens. This marks, in structural terms, the differentiation of the nuclear family from the extended family. (d) One aspect of this loss of control is the growth of personal choice, love, and related criteria as the basis for courtship and marriage. Correspondingly, marriage arranged by elders and extended kinsmen declines in importance. (e) One result of this complex of processes is the changing status of women, who become generally less subordinated economically, politically, and socially to their husbands than under earlier conditions. Frequently these developments are accompanied by feminist movements.

In such ways structural differentiation undermines the old modes of integration in society. The controls of extended family and village begin to dissolve in the enlarged and complicated social setting which differentiation involves. New problems are posed by this growing obsolescence of old integrative forms. We shall inquire presently into the emergence of new forms of integration.

Differentiation of Religious Systems

In Chapter 3 we noted that religious and nationalistic belief-systems vary in their effects on economic development. They may constitute a stimulus or an obstacle.[13] The logic of differentiation

[13] Above, pp. 41–42.

sociological aspects of economic development

permits us to account for these contrasting effects. In the early phases of development, for instance, many traditional loyalties may have to be broken in order to set up more differentiated social structures. Because these established commitments and methods of integration are deeply rooted in the organization of traditional society, a very generalized and powerful value commitment is often required to "pry" individuals from these attachments. The values of ascetic and this-worldly religious beliefs, xenophobic national aspirations, and political ideologies such as socialism provide such a lever. All three have an "ultimacy" of commitment in the name of which a wide range of sacrifices can be demanded and procured.

The very success of these value-systems, however, breeds the conditions for their own weakening. In a perceptive statement, Weber noted that by the beginning of the twentieth century, when the capitalistic system was already highly developed, it no longer needed the impetus of ascetic Protestantism.[14] Capitalism had, by virtue of its conquest of much of Western society, solidly established an institutional base and a secular value-system of its own—"economic rationality." These secular economic values no longer needed the "ultimate" justification required in the newer, unsteadier days of economic revolution.

The development of autonomous values such as economic rationality constitute the secularization of religious values. In this process, other institutional spheres—economic, political, scientific, etc.—come to be established on an independent basis. The values governing these spheres are no longer sanctioned directly by religious beliefs, but by autonomous rationalities. Insofar as such rationalities replace religious sanctions in these spheres, secularization occurs.

Similarly, nationalistic and related value-systems undergo a process of secularization as differentiation proceeds. As a society moves toward more and more complex social organization, diffuse nationalism gives way to more autonomous systems of rationality. The Soviet Union, for instance, as its social structure grows more differentiated, seems to be introducing more "independent" market mechanisms, "freer" social scientific investigation in some spheres, and so on. These measures are not, moreover, directly sanctioned by an appeal to nationalistic or communistic values.

Thus the paradoxical element in the role of religious or nationalistic values: Insofar as they encourage the breakup of old patterns, they may stimulate economic development; insofar as they resist their own subsequent secularization, however, the very same values may become a drag on economic advance and structural change.

Differentiation of Systems of Stratification

In discussing stratification in Chapter 3, we noted the importance of ascription-achievement in classifying ranking systems. We also asserted that collective forms of mobility (as opposed to individual mobility) are typically associated with ascribed systems of stratification.[15]

Many underdeveloped societies are characterized by ascribed systems of stratification and correspondingly by collective forms of mobility. Under

[14] *The Protestant Ethic and the Spirit of Capitalism* (London: Allen & Unwin, 1948), pp. 181–182.
[15] Above, pp. 65–67.

conditions of economic development, moreover, structural differentiation involves a change in both these characteristics:

1. Other evaluative standards intrude on ascribed memberships. For instance, McKin Marriott has noted that in the village of Paril in India,

> . . . Personal wealth, influence, and morality have surpassed the traditional caste-and-order alignment of kind groups as the effective bases of ranking. Since such new bases of ranking can no longer be clearly tied to any inclusive system of large solidary groupings, judgments must be made according to the characteristics of individual or family units. This individualization of judgments leads to greater dissensus (*sic*).[16]

Castes, ethnic groups, and traditional religious groupings do not necessarily decline in importance in every respect during periods of development. As we shall see presently, they may even increase in salience as political interest groups or reference groups for diffuse loyalty. As the sole bases of ranking, however, ascriptive standards become more differentiated from economic, political, and other standards.

2. Individual mobility through the occupational hierarchies increases. This signifies the differentiation of the adult's functional position from his point of origin. In addition, individual mobility is frequently substituted for collective mobility. Individuals, not whole castes or tribes, compete for higher standing in society. This phenomenon of increasing individual mobility seems to be one of the universal consequences of industrialization.[17] Patterns of class symbolization and class ideology, however, may continue to differ among industrialized countries.

The Integration of Differentiated Activities

One of Durkheim's insights concerned the role of integrative mechanisms under conditions of growing social heterogeneity. One of the concomitants of a growing division of labor (differentiation), he argued, is an *increase* in mechanisms to coordinate and solidify the interaction among individuals with increasingly diversified interests.[18] Durkheim located this integration mainly in the legal structure, but one can locate similar kinds of integrative forces elsewhere in society.

Differentiation alone, therefore, is not sufficient for modernization. Development proceeds as a contrapuntal interplay between differentiation (which is divisive of established society) and integration (which unites differentiated structures on a new basis). Paradoxically, however, the process of integration itself produces more differentiated structures—e.g., trade unions, associations, political parties, and a mushrooming state apparatus. Let us illustrate this complex process of integration in several institutional spheres.

Economy and Family

Under a simple kind of economic organization—subsistence agriculture or household industry—there is little differentiation between economic roles and family roles. All reside in the kinship structure.

---

[16] "Social Change in an Indian Village," *Economic Development and Cultural Change* (1952–1953), I: 153.
[17] Above, p. 67.
[18] Above, pp. 14–15.

The *integration* of these diverse but unspecialized activities also rests in the local family and community structures, and in the religious traditions which fortify both of these.

Under conditions of differentiation, the social setting for production is separated from that for consumption, and productive roles of family members are isolated geographically, temporally, and structurally from their distinctively familial roles. Such differentiation immediately creates integrative problems. How is information concerning employment opportunities to be conveyed to workpeople? How are the interests of families to be integrated with the interests of firms? How are families to be protected from market fluctuations? Whereas such integrative exigencies were faced by kinsmen, neighbors, and local largesse in pre-modern settings, development gives birth to dozens of institutions and organizations geared to these new integrative problems—labor recruitment agencies and exchanges, labor unions, government regulation of labor allocation, welfare and relief arrangements, cooperative societies, and savings institutions. All these involve agencies which specialize in integration.

Community

If industrialization occurs only in villages, or if villages are built around paternalistic industrial enterprises, many ties of community and kinship can be maintained under industrial conditions. Urbanization, however, frequently creates more anonymity. As a result of this anonymity we find in expanding cities a compensating growth of voluntary associations—churches and chapels, unions, schools, halls, athletic clubs, bars, shops, mutual aid groups, etc. In some cases this growth of integrative groupings may be retarded because of the back-and-forth movement of migratory workers, who "come to the city for their differentiation" and "return to the village for their integration." In cities themselves the original criterion for associating may be common tribe, caste, or village; this criterion may persist or give way gradually to more "functional" groupings based on economic or political interest.

Political Structure

In the typical pre-modern setting political integration is closely fused with kinship position, tribal membership, control of the land, or control of the unknown. Political forms include chieftanships, kingships, councils of elders, powerful landlords, powerful magicians and oracles, etc.

As social systems grow more complex, political systems are modified accordingly. Meyer Fortes and E. E. Evans-Pritchard have specified three types of African political systems, which can be listed according to their degree of differentiation from kinship lineages: (a) small societies in which the largest political unit embraces only those united by kinship; thus political authority is coterminous with kinship relations; (b) societies in which the political framework is the integrative core for a number of kinship lineages; (c) societies with an "administrative organization" of a more formal nature. Such systems move toward greater differentiation as population grows and economic and cultural heterogeneity increases.[19] In colonial and recently freed African societies, political systems have evolved

19 *African Political Systems* (London: Oxford University Press, 1940), pp. 1–25.

much further, with the appearance of parties, congresses, pressure groups, and even parliamentary systems. Sometimes this wider political integration, like community integration, is based on an extension and modification of an old integrative principle. Selig Harrison has argued, for instance, that modern developments in India have changed the significance of caste from the "traditional village extension of the joint family" to "regional alliances of kindred local units." This modification has led to the formation of "new caste lobbies" which constitute some of the strongest and most explosive political forces in modern India.[20] We shall mention some of the possible political consequences of this persistence of old integrative forms later.

Those examples illustrate how differentiation in society impinges on the integrative sphere. The resulting integrative structures coordinate and solidify—with varying success—the social structure which the forces of differentiation threaten to fragment. In many cases the integrative associations and parties display tremendous instability—labor unions turn into political or nationalistic parties; religious sects become political clubs; football clubs become religious sects, and so on.[21] The resultant fluidity points up the extremely pressing needs for re-integration under conditions of rapid, irregular, and disruptive processes of differentiation. The initial response is often a kind of trial-and-error floundering for many kinds of integration at once.

We have sketched some structural consequences of technological advance, agricultural commercialization, urbanization, and industrialization. We have analyzed these consequences in terms of differentiation and integration. The structural changes are not, it should be remembered, a simple function of "industrialization" alone. Some of the most far-reaching structural changes have occurred in countries which have scarcely experienced the beginnings of industrialization. For instance, colonialism—or related forms of economic dominance—creates not only an extensive differentiation of cash products and wage labor but also a vulnerability to world price fluctuations in commodities. Hence many of the structural changes described above—and many of the resulting social disturbances to be described presently—characterize societies which are still technically "pre-industrial."

Discontinuities in Differentiation and Integration: Social Disturbances

The structural changes associated with economic development are likely to be disruptive to the social order for the following reasons:

1. Differentiation demands the creation of new activities, norms, and sanctions—money, political position, prestige based on occupation, and so on. These often conflict with old modes of social action, which are frequently dominated by traditional religious, tribal, and kinship systems. These traditional standards are among the most intransigent of obstacles to modernization, and when they are threatened, serious dissatisfaction and opposition arise.

[20] *India: The Most Dangerous Decades* (Princeton: Princeton University Press, 1960), pp. 100 ff.
[21] Thomas Hodgkin, *Nationalism in Colonial Africa* (New York: New York University Press, 1957), pp. 85 ff.

sociological aspects of economic development

2. Structural change is, above all, *uneven* in periods of development. In colonial societies, for instance, the European powers frequently revolutionized the economic, political, and educational frameworks, but simultaneously encouraged or imposed a conservatism in traditional religious, class, and family systems.

> . . . The basic problem in these [colonial] societies was the expectation that the native population would accept certain broad, modern institutional settings . . . and would perform within them various roles—especially economic and administrative roles—while at the same time, they were denied some of the basic rewards inherent in these settings. . . . They were expected to act on the basis of a motivational system derived from a different social structure which the colonial powers and indigenous rulers tried to maintain.[22]

Under non-colonial conditions of development similar discontinuities appear. Within the economy itself, rapid industrialization, no matter how coordinated, bites unevenly into the established social and economic structure. And throughout the society, the differentiation occasioned by agricultural, industrial, and urban changes always proceeds in a see-saw relationship with integration; the two sets of forces continuously breed lags and bottlenecks. The faster the tempo of modernization, the more severe are the discontinuities.

3. Dissatisfactions arising from these discontinuities sometimes are aggravated by attempts to overcome them. Some discontinuities may be relieved in part by new integrative devices such as unions, associations, clubs, and government regulations. Such innovations are often opposed, however, by traditional vested interests because the new forms of integration compete with the older, undifferentiated systems of solidarity. The result is a three-way tug-of-war among the forces of tradition, the forces of differentiation, and the new forces of integration. Such conditions create virtually unlimited potentialities for the formation of conflicting groups.

Three classic responses to these discontinuities are anxiety, hostility, and fantasy. These responses, if and when they become collective, crystallize into a variety of social movements—peaceful agitation, political violence, millenarianism, nationalism, revolution, underground subversion, etc. There is plausible—though not entirely convincing—evidence that those drawn most readily into such movements are those suffering most severely the pains of displacements created by structural change. For example,

> [Nationalism appeared] as a permanent force in Southeast Asia at the moment when the peasants were forced to give up subsistence farming for the cultivation of cash crops or when (as in colonized Java) subsistence farming ceased to yield a subsistence. The introduction of a money economy and the withering away of the village as the unit of life accompanied this development and finally established the period of economic dependence.[23]

[22] S. N. Eisenstadt, "Sociological Aspects of Political Development in Underdeveloped Countries," *Economic Development and Cultural Change* (1956–1957), V: 298.

[23] Erich H. Jacoby, *Agrarian Unrest in Southeast Asia* (New York: Columbia University Press, 1949), p. 246.

Other theoretical and empirical evidence suggests that social movements appeal most to those who have been dislodged from old social ties by differentiation but who have not been integrated into the new social order.[24]

Many belief-systems associated with these movements envision the grand and almost instantaneous integration of society. In many cases the beliefs are highly emotional and unconcerned with realistic policies. In nationalistic colonial movements, for instance, "the political symbols were intended to develop new, ultimate, common values and basic loyalties, rather than relate to current policy issues within the colonial society." [25] Furthermore, such belief-systems reflect the ambivalence resulting from the conflict between traditionalism and modernization. Nationalists alternate between xenophobia and xenophilia; they predict that they will "out-modernize" the West in the future and simultaneously "restore" the true values of the ancient civilization; they argue for egalitarian and hierarchical principles of social organization at the same time.[26] Nationalistic and related ideologies unite these contradictory tendencies in a society under one large symbol; then, if these ideologies are successful, they are often used as a vehicle for further economic development.

Not all cases of development produce violent nationalistic or other social movements. When such movements do arise, furthermore, they take many different forms. The following factors seem to be the most decisive in the genesis and molding of social disturbances:

1. The scope and intensity of the social dislocation created by structural changes. "The greater the tempo of these changes . . . the greater the problems of acute malintegration the society has to face." [27]

2. The structural complexity of the society at the time when development begins. In the least developed societies, where "the language of politics is at the same time the language of religion," protest movements more or less immediately take on a religious cast. In Africa, for instance, utopian religious movements seem to have relatively greater appeal in the less developed regions, whereas the more secular types of political protest such as trade union movements and party agitations have tended to cluster in the more developed areas.[28] The secularization of protest increases as development and differentiation proceed.

3. The access of disturbed groups to channels of influencing social policy. If dislocated groups have access to those responsible for introducing reforms, agitation tends to be relatively peaceful and orderly. If this access is blocked, either because of the isolation of the groups or the intransigence of the ruling authorities, demands for reform tend to take more violent, utopian, and bizarre forms. Hence the tendency for fantasy and unorganized violence to cluster among the disinherited, the colonized, and the socially isolated migrants.

4. The overlap of interests and lines of cleavage. As we discovered

[24] William Kornhauser, The Politics of Mass Society (Glencoe, Ill.: The Free Press, 1959), Parts II and III; Seymour Martin Lipset, Political Man (Garden City, N. Y.: Doubleday, 1960), Chapter II.

[25] Eisenstadt, "Sociological Aspects of Political Development in Underdeveloped Countries," op. cit., p. 294.

[26] Mary Matossian, "Ideologies of Delayed Industrialization," Economic Development and Cultural Change (1957–1958), VI: 217–228.

[27] Eisenstadt, "Sociological Aspects of Political Development in Underdeveloped Countries, op. cit., p. 294.

[28] Hodgkin, op. cit., pp. 95–150.

114

above, those societies in which economic, political, and ethnic cleavages coincide are likely to produce more diffuse kinds of conflicts and social movements than societies in which these cleavages crisscross.[29]

5. The kind and extent of foreign infiltration and intervention on behalf of protest groups. Here we have tried to sketch, in ideal-type terms, the ways in which economic and social development is related to social structure. We have centered the discussion around three major concepts—differentiation, which characterizes a social structure moving toward greater complexity; integration, which in certain respects balances the divisive character of differentiation; and social disturbances, which result from the discontinuities between differentiation and integration.

To this analysis must be added four qualifications: (a) We have not attempted to account for the determinants of economic development itself. In fact, the discussion of differentiation, integration, and social disturbance takes as given a certain attempt to develop economically. These three forces, however, condition the *course* of development once it has started. (b) For purposes of exposition we have presented the three major categories in a certain order—differentiation, integration, social disturbances. We should not assume from this, however, that any one of them assumes causal precedence in the analysis of social change. Rather they form an interactive system. Disturbances, for instance, may arise from discontinuities created by structural differentiation, but these very disturbances may shape the course of future processes of differentiation. Likewise, integrative developments may be set in motion by differentiation, but in their turn they may initiate new lines of differentiation. (c) Even though the forces of differentiation, integration, and disturbance are closely linked empirically, we should not "close" the "system" composed of the relations among the three forces. Differentiation may arise from sources other than economic development; the requirement of integration may arise from conditions other than differentiation; and the sources of social disturbance are not exhausted by the discontinuities between differentiation and integration. (d) The "all-at-once" character of the transition from less differentiated to more differentiated societies should not be exaggerated. Empirically the process evolves gradually and influences the social structure selectively. The emphasis on various half-way arrangements and compromises throughout the chapter illustrates this gradualness and irregularity.

Structural Bases
for the Role of Government

We might end this chapter on a more policy-oriented note. Many have argued for the presence of a strong, centralized government in rapidly developing societies. Governmental planning and activity are required, for instance, to direct saving and investment, to regulate incentives, to encourage entrepreneurship, to control trade and prices, and so on.[30] To such arguments let us add several considerations arising from the analysis of structural change in periods of rapid development:

1. Undifferentiated institutional structures frequently constitute the primary social barriers to development. Individuals refuse to work for

[29] Above, p. 63.
[30] Joseph J. Spengler, "Social Structure, the State and Economic Growth," in Simon Kuznets, Wilbert E. Moore, and Joseph J. Spengler (eds.), *Economic Growth*, pp. 370–379.

wages because of traditional kinship, village, tribal, and other ties. Invariably a certain amount of political pressure is required to pry individuals loose from these ties. The need for such pressure increases, of course, with the rate of development desired.

2. The process of differentiation itself creates those conditions which demand a larger, more formal type of political administration. A further argument for the importance of government in periods of rapid and uneven development lies, then, in the need to accommodate the growing cultural, economic, and social heterogeneity, and to control the political repercussions arising from the constantly shifting distribution of power that accompanies extensive social reorganization.

3. The apparent propensity for periods of early development to erupt into explosive outbursts creates delicate political problems for the leaders of developing nations. What kinds of government are likely to be most effective in the face of these outbursts? First, political leaders will increase their effectiveness by open and vigorous commitment to utopian and xenophobic nationalism. This commitment serves as a powerful instrument for attaining three of their most important ends: (a) the enhancement of their own claim to legitimacy by endowing themselves with the mission for creating the nation-state; (b) the procurement of otherwise difficult sacrifices from a populace which may be committed to development in the abstract but which resists the concrete breaks with traditional ways; (c) the use of their claim to legitimacy to hold down protests and to prevent generalized symbols such as communism from spreading to all sorts of particular grievances. These same political leaders should not, however, take their enthusiasm for this claim to legitimacy too literally. They should not rely on the strength of their nationalistic commitment to ignore or smother grievances altogether. They should play politics in the usual sense with aggrieved groups in order to give these groups an access to responsible political agencies, and thereby reduce those conditions which give rise to counter-claims to legitimacy. One key to political stability would seem to be, therefore, the practice of flexible politics behind the facade of an inflexible commitment to a national mission.

Epilogue:
The Case for Economic Sociology

To close our account of the sociology of economic life, we shall indicate, in a few sentences, where we have been in this volume. We began with the notion that social life can be separated analytically into a number of "aspects"—the economic, the political, the legal, the religious, and so on. Even though analytically separable, however, these several aspects influence one another in the empirical world. In this volume we selected the economic aspect as a focus, but, unlike economists who often study this aspect in isolation, we elected to examine the interaction among the economic and non-economic aspects.

We began this examination by isolating some themes in the history of economic and social thought. Economic theorists, such as Adam Smith, Karl Marx, and John Maynard Keynes, ventured different assumptions about the relations between the economy and the rest of society. These assumptions often made a great difference in how these thinkers viewed the operation of the economy. Social theorists, such as Émile Durkheim, Max Weber, and Bronislaw Malinowski, systematically demonstrated how

sociological aspects of economic development

political, familial, and legal influences condition economic processes. Finally, economists and sociologists in modern times have begun to experiment with new theories and types of research to gauge the relations between economic and non-economic variables. The history of thought, then, presents a strong case for needing to observe the interaction among the several aspects of social life to gain an adequate account of any one aspect.

But this case, resting as it does on the unsystematic accumulation of thought of diverse writers through the ages, is only a very general case. It is necessary to become more specific and detailed in drawing out the interrelations between economic and non-economic variables. We attempted to introduce the detailed case for economic sociology in four ways:

1. We systematically compared the disciplines of the economist and the sociologist. We asked what kinds of assumptions each makes about the other's subject, what kinds of questions each asks in his own field, how each goes about answering these questions, how the fields overlap, and how they might be integrated theoretically.

2. We considered each aspect of social life as a sub-system of society. We then asked how each sub-system influenced and was influenced by the economy. Taking kinship as an example, we suggested that certain kinds of family structure have a greater "strain toward consistency" with wage and factory labor than other family structures. Turning to religion, we explored a major tradition of research on the effects of different religious beliefs on economic activity. Similarly, we reviewed the economic implications of research on the political system, the stratification system, etc.

3. We asked how non-economic variables condition various types of economic actions—production, distribution, and consumption. In this operation we incorporated many of the findings of industrial sociology, the research on comparative market structure, and the work of economists and sociologists on the determinants of spending and saving.

4. We asked how economic and non-economic variables affect one another during periods of social change. Concentrating on the problem of economic development, we first observed some of the ways that social factors facilitate or impede the effort to modernize. Then we showed how a rapidly developing economy brings about a proliferation of changes in the social structure. The case for economic sociology is particularly striking in the analysis of change, since many of the economists' simplifying assumptions are inapplicable when the economy's social environment is in flux.

An advantage of this multi-sided approach to the sociology of economic life is that we are able to locate the field's weaknesses as well as its strengths. We have discovered not only what we do know, but also what we do not know. We have attempted throughout to identify the gaps in our knowledge. As these gaps are filled gradually by the efforts of scholars, the field of economic sociology will come to play a unique and vital role, contributing to the development of both the fields it encompasses.

sociological aspects of economic development

selected references

These notes are intended to launch the student on a search through the available writings on economic sociology, rather than provide him a comprehensive bibliography.

For the discovery of sociological elements in economic thought, it is best to go through the classics. Important ones are Adam Smith, *Inquiry into the Nature and Causes of the Wealth of Nations* (New York: The Modern Library, 1937); Karl Marx, especially *Communist Manifesto* (London: Allen & Unwin, 1948, and many paperback editions), and *Capital* (New York: The Modern Library, 1936); Alfred Marshall, *Principles of Economics,* eighth edition, especially Books III and VI (New York: Macmillan, 1920); and John Maynard Keynes, *General Theory of Employment, Interest, and Money* (New York: Harcourt, Brace, 1936). An elementary secondary treatment of themes in the history of economic thought is Robert Lekachman, *A History of Economic Ideas* (New York: Harper, 1959). A more elaborate treatment is Overton H. Taylor, *A History of Economic Thought* (New York: McGraw-Hill, 1960). Joseph A. Schumpeter's *History of Economic Analysis* (New York: Oxford University Press, 1954) is an enormous and challenging work.

Classics in the history of sociological thought include the aforementioned works of Marx; Émile Durkheim, *The Division of Labor in Society,* translated by George Simpson (Glencoe, Ill.: The Free Press, 1949); Vilfredo Pareto, *The Mind and Society,* translated by Andrew Bongiorno and Arthur Livingston (New York: Harcourt, Brace, 1935); Max Weber, *The Protestant Ethic and the Spirit of Capitalism,* translated by Talcott Parsons (New York: Scribner, 1930), and *The Theory of Social and Economic Organization,* translated by A. M. Henderson and Talcott Parsons (New York: Oxford University Press, 1947). Of broad theoretical scope are Adolpe Löwe, *Economics and Sociology* (London: Allen & Unwin, 1935); Talcott Parsons, *The Structure of Social Action* (New York: McGraw-Hill, 1937); Talcott Parsons and Neil J. Smelser, *Economy and Society* (Glencoe, Ill.: The Free Press, 1956); and Karl Polanyi, C. M. Arensberg, and H. W. Pearson (eds.), *Trade and Market in the Early Empires* (Glencoe, Ill.: The Free Press, 1957).

Students interested in the economic life of non-industrial and non-market econo-mies should consult Bronislaw Malinowski's *Argonauts of the Western Pacific* (London: Routledge, 1922) and *Coral Gardens and Their Magic* (London: Allen & Unwin, 1935). Other sources are Marcel Mauss, *The Gift,* translated by Ian Cunnison (Glencoe, Ill.: The Free Press, 1954); Raymond Firth, *Primitive Polynesian Economy* (London: Routledge, 1939) and *Malay Fishermen* (London: Kegan Paul, Trench, Trubner, 1946). A recent effort to synthesize the field of economic anthropology is Melville J. Herskovits, *Economic Anthropology* (New York: Knopf, 1952).

In the field of industrial sociology, the single most significant work is F. J. Roethlisberger and William J. Dickson, *Management and the Worker* (Cambridge: Harvard University Press, 1947). The broader aspects of the "human relations" approach are explored in Elton Mayo, *The Social Problems of an Industrial Civilization* (Boston: Graduate School of Business Administration of Harvard University, 1945). Two leading texts in the area of industrial sociology are Wilbert E. Moore, *Industrial Relations and the Social Order,* revised edition, (New York: Macmillan, 1951); and Eugene V. Schneider, *Industrial Sociology* (New York: McGraw-Hill, 1957). The student interested in industrial conflict should refer to Arthur Kornhauser, Robert Dubin, and Arthur M. Ross (eds.), *Industrial Conflict* (New York: McGraw-Hill, 1954); and Walter Galenson and Seymour Martin Lipset (eds.), *Labor and Trade Unionism* (New York: Wiley, 1960). Journals specializing in labor studies are the *Industrial and Labor Relations Review,* and *Industrial Relations.*

For the sociological analysis of economic development, see Bert F. Hoselitz (ed.), *The Progress of Underdeveloped Areas* (Chicago: University of Chicago Press, 1952); Lyle B. Shannon (ed.), *Underdeveloped Areas* (New York: Harper's, 1957); Bert F. Hoselitz and Wilbert E. Moore (eds.), *Industrialization and Society* (The Hague: UNESCO-Mouton, 1963). The journal *Economic Development and Cultural Change* contains many studies of the social aspects of economic growth, as does the journal *Explorations in Entrepreneurial History.*

Other important volumes on various aspects of economic sociology are Reinhard Bendix, *Work and Authority in Industry* (New York: Wiley, 1956); Francis X. Sutton, *et al., The American Business Creed* (Cambridge: Harvard University Press, 1956); Adolph A. Berle and Gardiner C. Means, *The Modern Corporation and Private Property* (New York: Macmillan, 1933); Robert A. Gordon, *Business Leadership in the Large Corporation* (Washington, D. C.: Brookings Institute, 1945); Alvin W. Gouldner, *Patterns of Industrial Bureaucracy* (Glencoe, Ill.: The Free Press, 1954); and George Katona, *Psychological Analysis of Economic Behavior* (New York: McGraw-Hill, 1951). Journals containing many studies in economic sociology are *American Sociological Review, American Journal of Sociology, British Journal of Sociology,* and *American Journal of Economics and Sociology.*

118

index

120